Essential
Mallorca, Ibiza, Menorca

By
Tom Burns

Tom Burns is a journalist resident in Spain.
He is the principal contributor to the
Everything Under the Sun series of practical
guidebooks to Spain.

GW00362752

AA

Produced by AA Publishing

Written by Tom Burns
Peace and Quiet section
by Paul Sterry

First published January 1990
Revised second edition January
1995.
Reprinted March 1995
Reprinted August 1995

Edited, designed and produced
by AA Publishing.
© The Automobile Association
1995.
Maps © The Automobile
Association 1995.

Distributed in the United Kingdom
by AA Publishing, Norfolk House,
Priestley Road, Basingstoke,
Hampshire, RG24 9NY.

The contents of this publication
are believed correct at the time of
printing. Nevertheless, the
publishers cannot be held
responsible for any errors or
omissions or for changes in the
details given in this guide or for
the consequences of any reliance
on the information provided by
the same. Assessments of
attractions, hotels, restaurants and
so forth are based upon the
author's own experience and,
therefore, descriptions given in
this guide necessarily contain an
element of subjective opinion
which may not reflect the
publisher's opinion or dictate a
reader's own experience on
another occasion.
We have tried to ensure
accuracy in this guide, but
things do change and we would
be grateful if readers would
advise us of any inaccuracies
they may encounter.

Published by AA Publishing, a
trading name of Automobile
Association Developments
Limited, whose registered office
is Norfolk House, Priestley Road,
Basingstoke, Hampshire, RG24
9NY.
Registered number 1878835.

Colour separation: L.C. Repro,
Aldermaston

Printed by: Printers Trento, S.R.L.,
Italy

Front cover picture: *Cala Fornells,*
Mallorca

This book employs a simple rating system to help choose which places to visit:

✓	'top ten'

♦♦♦   do not miss
♦♦   see if you can
♦   worth seeing if you have time

The quiet side of the Balearics: dense greenery, white sands and deep blue seas

INTRODUCTION

In English they are known as the Balearic Islands or the Balearics; in Spanish they are *las Islas Baleares* or just *las Baleares*. There are three of them, or four if you count little Formentera, next to the island of Ibiza, and they are all distinct from each other; but taken together or separately, the Balearics/Baleares stand for leisure, sun and fun. They are geared for the holidaymaker, and they are Mallorca, Ibiza and Menorca.

The islands, to use all the right clichés, are the proverbial jewels set in the limpid, clear waters of the turquoise Mediterranean Sea; the description is no less true for being hackneyed. The operative word when describing the Balearics is Mediterranean; the islands enjoy the Mediterranean's enviable climate and they are scented with the Mediterranean smells of thyme and rosemary, and blessed with landscapes of almond trees, olive trees and vines.

The coastline offers the full range of Mediterranean possibilities: wide open beaches and rocky, secret coves. It is ideal for the sunsoaker and the sailor, the water-skier and the scuba diver. Such activities acquire a sort of cult status in the Balearics. Sun tans, for example, are taken very seriously in Ibiza where people have a tendency to show off their beautiful bodies. Sailing is an obsession for many people who have made the Balearics their permanent leisure home. The islands offer the right cruising mix of well-equipped resorts and marinas and solitary, hidden shores. The bay of Palma, moreover, has a nearly constant breeze which is ideal for international regattas. Windsurfing has, naturally, become a craze; and waterskiing and scuba diving always were crazes. The former includes the hang gliding and parachuting varieties while the latter is a religion for those who practise it. Landlubbers, of course, can view marine wonders in the Balearics courtesy of glass-bottomed boats.

Parts of the coast have become well-established holiday destinations. San Antonio in Ibiza or Magaluf in Mallorca are always crowded in the high season. For discos, aquaparks and bowling alleys thrown in with the junk food, such resorts are hard to beat, and certainly offer value for money.

Other parts of the Balearics are, however,

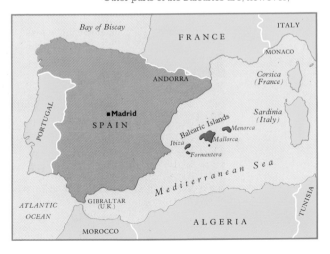

extremely unspoilt and this is one of the most surprising aspects of the islands. All that is required, if you want to have a cove to yourself, is a strong pair of legs and some local guidance to help you reach the inaccessible spots; but the easy way of doing it is to own or hire a yacht and approach such paradises by sea.

Still other parts of the islands are expensive and exclusive. The Spanish Royal Family spends its summers in Mallorca and cruises all round the Balearics with VIP guests such as the Prince of Wales aboard. The islands manage to be both the holiday playground for the charter flight masses and the watering

hole for celebrities. The Balearics are nothing if not varied at every level.

Mallorca is the biggest island in the archipelago and its capital, Palma de Mallorca, is the main town and the administrative centre of the Balearics. The island has a bit of everything – wide bays and tiny inlets, fertile, orchard-packed valleys, terraced hillsides and craggy peaks, crowds and concrete highrises, solitude and lonely, stone farmhouses. Many people leave Mallorca after their holidays without having ventured from the coast. This is a pity because inland Mallorca is delightful.

Windsurfing off the coast of Formentera; the sport has become hugely popular in the area

Shoppers browse near the Plaza Mayor in Palma de Mallorca

Palma is a bustling, busy, cosmopolitan city. Son San Juan, its international airport, works round the clock in the high season and its harbour hums all day. A Gothic cathedral and a medieval castle lend Palma historical interest and, with luxury shops crowding graceful boulevards and millionaire yachts packing the marina, the city is indisputably chic and classy.

Mallorca is a well-balanced island, in that although tourism is its foremost revenue earner it is by no means the area's sole economic activity. There is a well-developed shoe and leather goods industry; and a whole range of products, from furniture to cultured pearls, is manufactured on the island.

Menorca is the second biggest island and the most northerly of the group. It is similar to Mallorca insofar as it mixes high pressure resorts with rural arcadias; but the island is rather more blustery, and certainly more humid, without, on the whole, the high heat that Mallorca can undergo in July and August.

Another difference is the Englishness which Menorca can and does affect. This is difficult to pin down, until you start to take in the local architecture in greater detail, and start sampling the local punch-packing gin. Lattice windows and the good brew are the legacies of Britain's ownership of the island for part of the 18th century. The island was handed over to Britain by Spain, together with Gibraltar, in the 1713 Treaty of Utrecht, but unlike Gibraltar was returned to Spain before the end of the century.

Ibiza is, to be absolutely precise, not part of the Balearics. This island belongs, together with its tiny satellite isle, Formentera, to a different archipelago which goes under the name of the Islas Pitiusas. Yet as far as 20th-century travellers and guide books are concerned, lovely, dry and whitewashed Ibiza and its nearby semi-desert island of Formentera are part and parcel of the Baleares.

Just as Menorca receives the wetter north winds, Ibiza, which lies below Mallorca, has hot, African breezes and is very much drier. The glowing whiteness of Ibiza's functional-looking architecture, the exotic atmosphere of Ibiza town, places it nearer the African continent than Europe.

That said, Ibiza is, like its sister isles, Mediterranean through and through. This is the land of the fig, of the almond tree, of the vine and of a wild and pungent *bouquet garni* of rosemary, thyme, basil and marjoram. Where Ibiza is different is in its 'anything goes' attitude to life. The island is so laid back, you would think it never moved; and yet it can be so hyper-active under outrageous disco strobes that you would think it was never still. *Aficionados* of Ibiza say the place is more of a state of mind than a geographical location. There is something surreal about having, as Ibiza does, a monument dedicated to the *Corsario*, or the Pirate, whose base Ibiza was in the 18th century.

Something for Everybody

The Balearics are an archipelago with a long history behind them. Like all other Mediterranean islands they are a crucible and a melting pot of the different civilisations that have dominated that sea since antiquity. Proud of their own distinctive, carefully evolved culture, the Balearics are nevertheless wide open and welcoming to outsiders.

A cynic would say that these islands receive visitors because they make a fortune from the holiday trade. That would be unfair. There is a genuine warmth towards outsiders and a terrific tolerance towards those whose customs clash with the islanders' own. It would he truer to say that the Balearics have made a fine art out of living with invaders (and 20th-century mass tourism is a modern form of invasion), because the islands have learnt to mould those who arrive into accepting Balearic lifestyles and standards. What you now find on the Balearics is people from all over the world doing more or less the same things. The islands have long been turned over to the holidaymaking idea. The range of activities and attractions on offer is staggering, and the ways of enjoying them are manifold. But what is actually being done boils down to the simple exercise of forgetting work and winter worries.

There are, dotted around the archipelago, places which are the last word in elegance, and areas providing cheap, boisterous home-from-home holidays. The essential point is probably that you can be yourself and do what you like on these islands. There is room for the sedate and for the pace-setters of the next century. And that is the measure of the Balearics' wide appeal.

Modern Spain

One thing which may surprise you on arrival at the Balearics is that the locals speak Mallorquin, a language that is quite different from Spanish, as well as Spanish itself; and that signs, road signs included, will be in both languages. Thus Ibiza, which is the name of the island in Spanish, or to be precise in

Castilian Spanish, is also rendered as Eivissa, which is the island's name in Mallorquin. The Balearics have one distinctive feature in their language; it is basically a dialect of the Catalan, which is·spoken in the autonomous community of Catalonia, the northeast corner of mainland Spain which is centred on Barcelona. Another feature is an easy going and open nature, which is the heritage of the Mediterranean basin and which contrasts with, say, the proud and austere character of the Castilian.

An essential fact to grasp about Spain today is that it is a quasi-federal nation; the Balearic Islands form an autonomous unit within the Spanish state and they have wide ranging powers of home rule which are exercised by the regional government and by the regional parliament of the Balearic Islands. The

The appeal of beaches such as this one on Ibiza has triggered off the modern 'invasion' of tourists

Balearics are one of the 17 autonomous communities, known in Spanish as *Comunidades Autonomas*, that together make up modern Spain.

Decentralisation has been part and parcel of the restoration both of democracy and of the monarchy in Spain that followed the death of General Francisco Franco in 1975. Franco had ruled Spain as a one party state following his victory in the 1936–39 Spanish Civil War. He was succeeded by King Juan Carlos, the grandson of Alfonso XIII, who left Spain in 1931 when a republic was proclaimed; the republic was to be squashed five years later by Franco's military rebellion.

The autonomous framework of contemporary Spain reflects the very marked regional differences of the country. Spain, some say, is really plurinational. You will notice this in the Balearics: for example, there are a number of Basque restaurants on the islands, for Basque cooking is very highly rated and the cuisine of that autonomous community is very distinctive. Similarly, regional differences are marked by folklore. Flamenco, to cite an obvious case, is not Spanish folklore, nor is it Balearic folklore, but that of the autonomous community of Andalucia, the southern belt of mainland Spain.

Spain today is a constitutional monarchy with a parliamentary system, and a member of the European Community and of NATO. Spain is the largest country in the European Community after France and is twice the size of Britain at 195,000 square miles (505,000 sq km); but it comes fifth in the population table (almost 40 million). Parts of mainland Spain are extremely sparsely populated; in the Balearics population density is higher, though less than is the norm in northern Europe. Economically, Spain is grouped with the poorer European Community nations. Spain's per capita GDP in 1987 was \$7,410. The Spanish economy is, however, growing very fast, at between 4-5 per cent per annum, which is double the European Community average. The Balearics are both the richest and the fastest growing of Spain's autonomous communities.

BACKGROUND AND HISTORY

The Balearic Islands are a true melting pot of Mediterranean civilisations. If you could peel off the cultural layers of the average islander you would be working your way back to Muslims, Romans, Carthaginians, Greeks and Phoenicians.

The golden age of the Balearics came and went in the 14th century, which was when the islands formed part of a medieval Spanish kingdom based on the mainland provinces of Catalonia and Aragón. This was a proper Mediterranean kingdom, for its possessions stretched across to Sicily, southern Italy and beyond.

Half a millennium ago the Balearics had a merchant navy of some 900 vessels and the Mediterranean was a sort of back yard for the islands' 30,000 seamen. The men from the Balearics plied up and down the Mediterranean from Cadiz to Constantinople and the charts produced by the islands' highly respected school of cartography were prized objects.

Prehistory and the Bronze Age

The earliest signs of human habitation on the Balearics date from 4,000-3,000BC and were found in what is called the Muleta cave near the town of Sóller in Mallorca. In around 1,200BC what is known as the Talayot culture set down roots both in Mallorca and in

Sóller, on Mallorca – an example of a town which still has a sense of the past, despite being a resort

Menorca. There is a well-preserved Talayot settlement called Capocord Vell near the town of Llucmayor in Mallorca, and there are more good remains near Artá, at the eastern end of Mallorca's Bahia de Alcudia.

Here and there on these two islands you will come across evidence of this Bronze Age culture. There are remains of watchtowers, which are known as *Talayots* after the people who built them; there are sacrificial altars called *Taulas* – which means table in the Mallorcan language; and there are, particularly in Menorca, vestiges of burial chambers called *Navetas*, or boats, because they look like upside-down vessels. In Formentera, near San Fernando there is a megalithic sepulchre called Can Na Costa.

Greeks and Romans

After visits by Greeks and by Phoenicians, who set up trading stations and small colonies on the islands, it was the turn of the Romans. The legions of Quintilia Cecilius Metelos conquered Mallorca in 123BC and founded the city of Palma. Roman civilisation was to leave a lasting cultural imprint on Mallorca and Menorca, as it was on all Spain. Spain is second only to Italy in the wealth of its Roman remains. Ibiza, in contrast, resisted the Romans and was never formally conquered by them. The island remained a Carthaginian stronghold even after Hannibal's defeat in the second Punic war. African culture remained for centuries here in customs, language and beliefs. In the 5th century Ibiza was settled by Arabs, a good 300 years before the Muslim invasion of Spain and 500 years before they moved Islam into Mallorca and Menorca. Ibiza's separate development shows today, for it is 'African' in a way that Mallorca and Menorca are not.

Unfortunately nothing at all remains physically of Roman Palma. You will, however, find the ruins of a Roman theatre in Alcudia, Mallorca, where there was a fair-sized settlement called Pollentia. In the 5th century Roman civilisation crumbled in the Balearics and in Spain, just as it did

everywhere else. Vandals tried to colonise Mallorca and the island entered the Dark Ages with a vengeance. The Balearics as a whole became little more than a string of pirate bases.

The Moorish Period

The Moors, who invaded and overran mainland Spain in AD711, finally arrived on Mallorca and Menorca in AD903, which is when what remained of the city that the Romans had called Palma was renamed Medina Mayurqa. Islam was to remain present in mainland Spain until 1492 when its last stronghold, the Kingdom of Granada, fell to the Christian forces of Isabella of Castile and Ferdinand of Aragón. The Balearics, however, were 'liberated' much earlier. The Christian recovery of Spain, known as the *Reconquista*, or reconquest, is the fulcrum of Spanish history.

The Islamic occupation of the Balearics was marked by tolerance and was wholly beneficial. Palma/Mayurqa became an important town of some 25,000 inhabitants and water wells and irrigation methods, introduced by the sophisticated Arab settlers, helped to create a proper agricultural base for the island. Again, little remains of the Moorish period. The islands were conquered, and pretty much razed to the ground, by Christian troops led by James I of Aragón in 1229. The only Muslim traces left in Palma are the Arabian Baths, the Almudaina arch and a wing of the Ca'n Solleric, a building which nowadays houses the City Art Hall.

Medieval and Modern

The Balearics now came under the total influence of Barcelona on the mainland, and acquired the Catalan language which is known on the islands as Mallorquin. Within a century of its conquest Palma, with its sparkling new docks, its Gothic cathedral and its Bellver Castle, was to become an important Mediterranean trading centre. The Kingdom of Aragón, which had conquered the Balearics, encompassed the greater part of northern and eastern Spain, including Catalonia and the Valencia region; and its possessions were to extend across the Mediterranean to Naples and beyond. The Balearics, and Mallorca in particular, were strategically useful for what was, in its golden age, a considerable

Even the ancient Drach Caves on Mallorca have entered the tourists' world, with light and sound effects

Mediterranean power.

In the late 15th century the crowns of Castile and Aragón united through the marriage of Isabella and Ferdinand, and Spain was to acquire its present-day modern frontiers when in 1492 the Catholic Kings conquered Granada, Islamic Spain's last remaining bastion. Castile was, in time, to gain ascendancy over the Aragonese element in the unified monarchy and, with the discovery and conquest of the New World, which was spearheaded by Castilians, Spain's interest as a nation shifted from the Mediterranean to the Atlantic. By the late 16th century, the Balearics, former key posts in Aragón's maritime empire, were entering a period of genteel decline.

Piracy

Coastal commerce, fishing and agriculture were to remain staple Balearic businesses with occasional hiccups brought on by plundering pirates. All over the Balearics you will see

BACKGROUND

fortified churches and houses, and watchtowers – sure evidence that piracy was a real threat. The towns and villages in the Balearics tended to be built prudently back from the coast and from possible pirate raids; in fact coastal development in the Balearics is only some 30 years old. Before that there were only makeshift jetties and fishermen's cottages on the Balearic shoreline.

One of the most notorious of the archipelago's pirates, a 15th-century gentleman named Redbeard, had his base camp on the rocky isle of Sa Dragonera just off western Mallorca. On the other side of the island current tourist magnets such as the caverns, or the Cuevas del Drach were pirate residences.

The Latest Invasion

The Balearics were most recently invaded by those of us who have 'discovered' the

Chopin's links with Mallorca are cherished in the Charterhouse in Valldemosa

islands in the latter half of the 20th century. From the late 1950s onwards the face of the Balearics has undergone an astonishing change, powered by the age of mass travel. Again and again you will come across those who will say they knew as a fishing village the place which is now a high-powered resort, teeming with night life.

Precursors of the present invasion were the Romantics of the last century, such as the Austrian aristocrat Archduke Luis Salvador of Hapsburg-Lorena and Bourbon, who bought estates in northern Mallorca; and Frédéric Chopin, who spent a seminal winter in the Mallorcan village of Valldemosa.

Virtually until the present day the Balearics remained a shared and beautiful Mediterranean secret among select foreigners. One such was the poet Robert Graves who made his home in Deiá, near the Archduke's estates, when he said *Goodbye to All That* after World War I.

MALLORCA

It is still possible to enjoy areas of natural coastline on Mallorca, as yet untouched by the tourist industry's resort developments

The largest of the Balearic Islands, Mallorca is not exactly big. It measures 62 miles (100km) east to west at its widest point, from Cala Ratjada to Puerto de Andraitx; and 47 miles (75km) from the Cabo Formentor in the north to Cabo de Salinas in the south. In Palma and Manacor it has the two largest population centres on the Balearic Islands, with 316,000 and 27,500 inhabitants respectively.

The island looks as if two large bites have been taken out of it to form the Bahia de (bay of) Alcudia in the northeast and the Bahia de Palma in the southwest. The Sierra de Tramontana mountain range shields the island from northerly winds and creates the rocky headlands and the cliffs of the northwest coast. The centre of the island is its flattest area, and the land level tapers down to the depression of the Bahia de Alcudia.

Tourism is obviously Mallorca's major income earner, but the island is not wholly dependent on mass tourism. The terraced

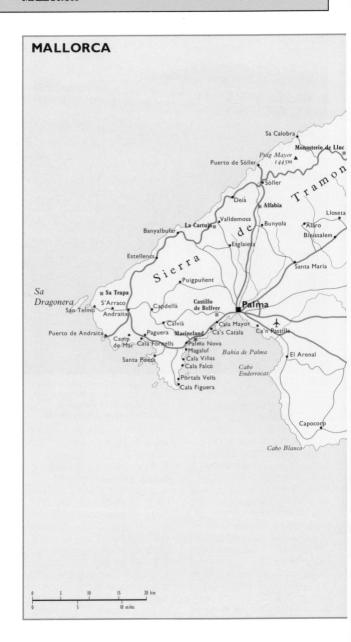

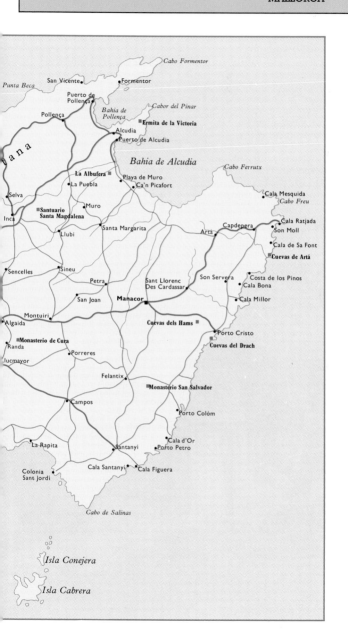

farming of inland Mallorca, laid out more than 1,000 years ago, still produces varied crops, and the island is one of Spain's main shoe manufacturing areas. Palma is a major services centre and the political capital of the Balearics. The government and the parliament of the Autonomous Community of the Balearic Islands are based in Palma, and key decisions concerning urban planning, tourism and transport are made by these regional bodies.

It would be a pity if you were to stay close by your resort during your Mallorcan sojourn. The island is very varied and is by no means crowded and built up everywhere. Exploring Mallorca's byways is utterly rewarding. The main recompense is that you will be discovering for yourself hidden coves and beaches which even the tourist authorities may not know about.

You should also consider taking a boat tour. Virtually every resort is served by steamers that ply up and down the coast. The idea is that the boat drops passengers off on

coves, which are virtually inaccessible by land, in the morning and picks them up in the afternoon.

One of the pleasantest trips on Mallorca is the narrow gauge railway which links Palma to Sóller on the northwest coast.

PALMA DE MALLORCA

Palma de Mallorca, capital of Mallorca island and of the Balearics as a whole, is a large,

Palma's cathedral, dating from the 13th century, towers impressively over the city and its harbour

sophisticated and cosmopolitan city. If you have never been there think of it as a mix of Marseilles, Naples and Nice. Set on its beautifully sheltered bay, Palma is the administrative and bureaucratic base for the whole archipelago; it is the headquarters of the Balearics tourism industry; it is an important maritime centre, and it is home to top hotels, restaurants, nightclubs and celebrities.

Palma was founded by the Romans; it became a key Muslim city and it grew in importance after its conquest by Christian forces in the 13th century and its incorporation into the Kingdom of Aragón. The city has always been a Mediterranean crossroads and you should be able to discern the Italianate influences that its architecture acquired during its boom 14th- and 15th-century years.

The city has three distinct areas. There is an old quarter which was walled in until the beginning of this century and which centres on the cathedral. This area is called, in Spanish, the *Casco Viejo*, or Old Town.

Then there is the new modern city stretching out westwards along the bay. The third area is the harbour and promenade area, the *Paseo Marítimo*, directly below the cathedral and on the bay itself. The harbour is a forest of masts; Palma's bay is said to contain the highest concentration of yachts and pleasure vessels in the Mediterranean.

To get Palma's full scope you must take a boat ride out into the bay and take time to remain out there when dusk sets in. That is when the harbour and boat lights start twinkling and the cathedral and Bellver Castle become illuminated. There is nothing quite like approaching Palma and its bay by sea.

WHAT TO SEE

◆◆
ARABIAN BATHS
Calle Serra
The Baths are the sole important trace left of Islam's presence on the island. Watch out for the tell-tale horseshoe arches in the main square chamber. The horseshoe design was perfected by the Moors during their long sojourn in Spain. The first Moorish invasion took place in 711, and the last Moorish bastion, the Kingdom of Granada, was regained by the Spanish in 1492.

◆◆
ALMUDAINA PALACE
Palau Reial
An arch still stands here from the old Moorish edifice; but the rest of the building, which is partly a museum and partly a Naval Command HQ, was built in the reign of James II, the Christian ruler of Mallorca in the 14th century.
For an inkling of what the traditional, albeit grand, Mallorcan patio used to look like, visit the City Art Hall, housed in the 18th-century Ca'n Solleric, a magnificent town mansion.

◆◆◆
BELLVER CASTLE ✔
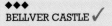

Parque de Bellver
The name of this castle, which, like the cathedral is a great Palma landmark, means 'fine view' in Catalan. It is well-named. Built in the early 15th century, the castle is one of the better kept and more impressive fortifications on the Mediterranean. Originally a royal palace, it was later a prison, and is now the **Municipal History Museum**. For Spaniards, the most interesting part of the castle is the frightful dungeon where the enlightened 18th-century reformist **Gaspar Melchor Jovellanos**, a sort of Spanish Voltaire, was imprisoned when he fell foul of absolutist Bourbon kings. Other visitors may be more interested in the graffiti scratched out in other dungeons by Napoleonic officers captured by the Duke of Wellington's troops during the Peninsular War.
Closed: Sundays

◆◆◆
CATHEDRAL ✔

Palau Reial
Palma's cathedral, which is known as La Seo (a Catalan term meaning a bishop's see), is worth a detailed visit. The cathedral combines an original Romanesque layout with later Gothic architecture, for although the foundation stone was laid in 1230, the building was not completed until 1601. At the beginning of the century the famed Barcelona modernist architect, Antonio

The courtyard of Bellver Castle, which in its time has been a palace and a prison. Now visitors come to admire the architecture

Gaudi, was responsible for restoration work.

The immediately striking feature of the cathedral is sheer size and the manner in which the whole mass is supported by slender and soaring pillars. The rose window above the presbytery is said to be one of the largest in the world and measures 43½ft (13.3m) in diameter. Note the bishop's marble pulpit in the presbytery, which has the unusual addition of tapestries, and then examine the wonderfully delicate 15th-century carvings that decorate the choir stalls.

The highpoint of the **Cathedral Museum** is a solid silver tabernacle used for ceremonial processions. Other exhibits include early 15th-century religious paintings, vestments and liturgical ornaments, ecclesiastical manuscripts and a particularly fine pair of 18th-century candelabra.

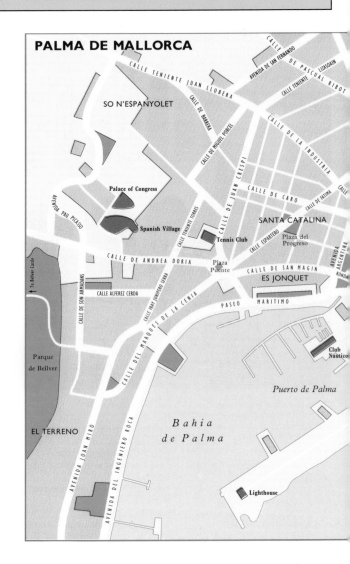

PALMA DE MALLORCA

CALLE TENIENTE JUAN LLOBERA

AVENIDA DE SAN FERNANDO

CALLE DE PASCUAL RIBOT

CALLE TENIENTE LIZASOAIN

SO N'ESPANYOLET

CALLE DE BARRERA

CALLE DE MIGUEL PORCEL

CALLE DE LA INDUSTRIA

CALLE DE JUAN CRESPI

CALLE DE CARO

CALLE DE FATIMA

CALLE

AVENIDA PAU PICASSO

Palace of Congress

SANTA CATALINA

Spanish Village

CALLE TENIENTE TORRES

Tennis Club

Plaza del Progreso

CALLE ESPARTERO

AVENIDA ARGENTINA

To Bellver Castle

CALLE DE ANDREA DORIA

Plaza Puente

CALLE DE SAN MAGIN

AVENIDA RONDA

CALLE DE SON ARMADANS

ES JONQUET

CALLE ALFEREZ CERDA

CALLE FRAY JUNIPERO SERRA

PASEO MARITIMO

Parque de Bellver

CALLE DEL MARQUES DE LA CENIA

Club Nautico

Puerto de Palma

EL TERRENO

AVENIDA JOAN MIRO

AVENIDA DEL INGENIERO ROCA

Bahia de Palma

Lighthouse

◆◆
CHURCH OF SAN FRANCISCO

Plaza San Francisco

Anyone interested in architecture and European art should be pleased by this lovely Gothic building. Built during the 13th century, it has an outstanding high altarpiece typical of the baroque exuberance which took Spain by storm during the course of the 17th century.

The choir stalls were carved in the 15th century. San Francisco is the site of the **tomb of Ramón Llul**, a fascinating Mallorcan who was an Erasmus-type figure in the 12th century. Llul was a mystic-cum-theologian-cum-philosopher, and an inveterate traveller around the Mediterranean. His learning was highly respected and opened doors to the mightiest powers wherever he went. He was a long way ahead of his time: he assembled information and set it down in an encyclopaedia; he wrote long narrative tracts about city life long before the novel was invented; and he was fascinated by language, and invented a number of words for the (then patchy) Catalan idiom.

◆◆
THE LONJA

Paseo Sagrera

One of several buildings in old Palma which are worth a closer inspection, the Lonja was used as the city's Exchange, and is an interesting example of extremely sober Gothic civil art. It was built in the 15th century and is now used for art

Traces of Muslim influence from the Islamic occupation can still be found in the Almudaina Palace

exhibitions (closed Mondays). Nearby the **Consulado del Mar**, a one-time judiciary that ruled on maritime trade and now the seat of the Regional Government of the Balearics, has a stunning second floor gallery (not open to the public).

Accommodation

If you plan to arrive in high season (July to September and the week before and after Easter) it is vital to book ahead. There is ample choice of hotels in Palma, but the tops of the town are without a doubt the

Son Vida (tel: 790000) in the Urbanización Son Vida and the **Valparaiso Palace**, Calle Francisco Vidal 33 (tel: 400411), which is in an area called La Bonanova. If you are especially sporty you might like the **Racquet Club Son Vida**, Urbanización Son Vida (tel: 280050), and if you want to be near the Paseo Maritimo try the **Sol Palas Atenea**, Paseo Ingeniero Gabriel Roca 29 (tel: 281400), and the rather more old fashioned **Meliá Victoria**, Avenida Joan Miró 2 (tel: 732542). At the scenic Ca's Català, km 7 on the road to Andraitx, stands the very agreeable and family run **Maricel** hotel (tel: 402712).

Nightlife
Palma in the high season is pretty much a constant party. Pre-dinner drinks are imbibed on the terraces and in the cafés on the Paseo del Borne and on the Plaza de la Lonja. After dinner action moves to the discos, pubs and bars in or near the Plaza de la Gomila. The El Arenal area particularly attracts British crowds, and there is, in addition, a string of discos on Avenida Son Rigo. An alternative is to stick to the Paseo Maritimo, home of entertainment milestones such as the very ritzy **Club de Mar** and the slightly highbrow **Jazz Piano Bar**. You can gamble all you want, as long as you take your passport with you, at the **Casino Sporting Club Mallorca**, which is in the Urbanización Sol de Mallorca, Magaluf.

Restaurants
Palma is packed with eating places of every variety. They include the good, the bad, and the plain fast food. Don't forget that there are excellent roadside inns called *fondas*, where you will perhaps get better value for money, and will certainly meet fewer crowds. Small, no-frills bars are called *cellers* and they serve tapas, bar snacks which have pride of place in every self-respecting Spanish bar. They are widely varied and usually include potato omelette, stewed kidneys, clams, mussels and shrimps, Russian salad, spicy sausages and cured ham. The top restaurant in Palma is generally considered to be

Porto Pi, Avenida Joan Miró 174; this is a turn-of-the-century mansion and is Basque-cuisine inspired. It also goes in for imagination and modernity. A meal here will delight the gourmet but can be quite expensive. **Caballito del Mar**, just across from the Lonja in the centre of the fishing harbour, offers great local fish cooking and rice dishes. **Ca'n Nofre**, Héroes de Manacor 27, is a popular eating house which specialises in the island fare, including *caldo de arroz a la marinera*, a fish and seafood broth to which rice is added; *caldereta de langosta*, lobster stewed in tomato sauces with green peppers and onions, and *tumber*, a vegetable dish of aubergines, courgettes,

potatoes and sweet red peppers. **Xoriguer**, Calle Fábrica 60, is not easy to find, but worth it; inventive and fun but authentic. The street is near the Plaza del Progreso, behind the beginning of the Paseo Maritimo promenade.

Out of town, try **Sa Sinia** in Calle Pescadores 5, Porto Colóm, Felantix which is well worth a day's outing. It is a stone vault cellar across from the marina that packs in people who like it as much for its atmosphere as for its cooking. Also **Ca'n Perdiueta**, Portals Nous, on the other side of

During the holiday season Palma's nightlife springs into action, with entertainment ranging from smart clubs to crowded discos

Palma Bay at Calvià: this is an unfussy fishermen's den serving a selection of tasty Mediterranean feasts.

Shopping
Palma has just about everything for the shopper. *The* department store, if you are in a hurry, is **Galerías Preciados** in Avenida Rey Jaime III. You will see local products such as hand-blown glass, cultured pearls, costume jewellery, ceramics and embroidery. You will also obtain an inkling of Spanish fashions, which could be a revelation.

If you are seriously interested in shopping you will want to spend time exploring the Avenida Rey Jaime III and the Paseo del Borne and the side streets leading off them. A selection of the shops there indicates the variety of goods to be found: **Arte España**, Paseo Mallorca 17: excellent for antiques, crafts and gifts in general. **Loewe**, Paseo del Borne 2: very upmarket fashion and leather goods, **Majórica**, Avenida Rey Jaime III, is the place to look for the cultured pearl. **Yanko**, Calle Unió 3, is good for a wide selection of shoes and **La Montaña**, Calle Jaime 29, is a gourmet shop that sells most of the local delicacies.

There is a Saturday flea-market from 08.00 to 14.00 hrs at the Avenida Gabriel Alomar i Villalonga where you just might, but almost certainly won't, find the art object that will make you independently wealthy; and at the street market in the Plaza Mayor a number of stalls sell a varied range of handicrafts Monday, Friday and Saturday. In these places beware of pickpockets.

Sports
Sailing is the premier sport in Palma and the yacht clubs are down in the harbour. Landlubbers can learn to sail at the Escuela de Vela de Cala Nova, Avenida Joan Miró, and they can start scuba diving after contacting the Centro de Actividades Subacuaticas Tritón, which is at Roger de Lluria 4A.

Most hotels and holiday centres have fairly complete sports facilities and will have information on sailing, windsurfing, waterskiing and the rest. The Son Vida complex, on the Son Rapila road just out of town, is in the premier division and has a golf course, a riding school, and tennis courts. You really need to get well away from Palma if you want a proper swim in the sea. The nearest beaches (Ca'n Pastilla and El Arenal, east of the city, and Cala Mayor, southwest), are well equipped and have good sand, but in high season tend to be standing room only.

PALMA NOVA AND MAGALUF

Just 9 miles (14km) from Palma city, following the Bahia de Palma southwest, you come to Palma Nova and Magaluf, cheek by jowl. These are the sort of places that not only keep charter airlines and tour operators in business but make them fortunes as well. This is not the place where you will find much peace and quiet – nor much that is authentically Mallorcan, let alone Spanish. This is the concrete jungle of pizza parlours and discos where everything from food to friendship is fast.

This is the favoured resort of young tourists, who arrive by the jumbo load and head straight for bars and pubs. If you have little time for youthful exuberance avoid Magaluf in general and its neon light areas in particular. If, on the other hand, you like cavorting around in noisy gangs then this is very much the place for you. In winter the whole scene changes as senior citizens occupy the hotels and apartment blocks which the boisterous brigade invades in summer. These winter holidays are becoming increasingly popular and rightly so. The prices are of the bargain basement variety and the weather can be exceedingly mild.

WHAT TO SEE

◆◆
CALVIÁ COAST

The two linked resorts of Palma Nova and Magaluf belong to what is properly called the Calviá coastline, an area in southwest Mallorca. There are all of 32 coves and six beaches along this 31-mile (50km) stretch of mostly jagged coast. The municipal centre, as it were, of this resort area, is the old city of Calviá, which lies inland. It is here, at the town hall, that you will receive all the relevant information for Magaluf, Palma Nova and beyond.

The Calviá area includes arguably some of Mallorca's best beauty spots (unspoilt coves which you have to reach by sea) and indisputably some of its worst eyesores (the two resorts under discussion which are easily reached by charter flights). It stretches from Cas' Català Beach on the bay of Palma to Cala Fornells, just west of the Bay (Cas', a Mallorcan word, originally meant 'small house'; Ca'n, often seen in place-names, denotes a larger house).

For unspoilt coves try **Es Caló d'en Monjo**, **Figuera** and **Sa Nostra Dona**. There are nudist beaches in the latter cove and there is more skinny-dipping on the **El Mago** beach; **Cala Falcó** and **Calas Portals Vells**, where there are interesting caves, are not exactly wild, but nor have they been blighted by mass tourism. The **El Sec Islet** is great for underwater exploring.

◆
MAGALUF BEACH

This is the longest beach on the Calviá coast, but it is nevertheless chock-a-block come the first week in August. The beach, in fact, keeps growing thanks to imported sand. Of all the resorts in Mallorca this is the place for knock-about fun.

If you spend any time here you will inevitably find yourself searching around the cheap leather goods stores of Ca'n Joan; sliding and splashing about at the Aquapark (very

Sun-worshippers prepare for a long day's lazing on Magaluf Beach

high chutes here); and speeding around the track of Karting Magaluf.

◆◆
PALMA NOVA BEACH
There are, in fact, three beaches here: Palma Nova I, Palma Nova II and Son Maties, and they each form a distinct sector of the resort.

The yacht club and the wind surfing school are on Palma Nova I. When you enter the next sector, Palma Nova II, you will probably agree with most people that this is the best beach in the resort. It has all the facilities one could wish for. Son Maties is fairly sporty with lots of waterskiing and wind surfing. The old round watchtower at the end of the beach marks the division between Palma Nova and Magaluf. Son Maties is very energetic in the evening when the bars, hamburger joints and discos are teeming.

Local excursions can offer alternative attractions:
Cala Viñas, south of Magaluf. Quieter and more family-orientated. There is a fairly good hotel here, Forte Cala Viñas, and there is total peace and solitude further south at Cala Falcó and by the nudist Bella Dona area.

Costa d'en Blanes, north of Palma Nova is a relaxing and well-equipped resort. Attractions here include the dolphins at **Marineland** and the chance to get a tan in double quick time at the **Son Calíu** cove which is a famed, strategically situated sun trap.

Accommodation
Hotels are as a rule booked solid by tour operators. Among the best in Magaluf are: **Atlantic**, Punta Ballena (tel: 680208), **Sol Coral Playa**, Sotavento 41 (tel: 680562) and the **Magalluf Playa**, Avenida Notario Alemany 1 (tel: 131050). In Palma Nova: **Comodoro Sol**, Paseo Calablanca (tel: 680200) and the **Delfín Playa Sol**, Hermanos Moncada 29 (tel: 680100).

Nightlife
If you are in Magaluf-Palma Nova and do not go to **Barrabás** and **Borsalsino** you really have chosen the wrong resort. These two Palma Nova discos are the stuff of legend and there are people who spend more of their holiday time under their strobes than under the sun.

Restaurants
This is fast food country and there is a perpetual reek of mustard, relish and frying fat to the place. **Ciro's**, marking the boundary between Palma Nova I and II sectors, is an exception that proves the rule. It is a pleasant terrace restaurant with a good view of the sea and the sun soakers. It does, like everything else in the area, get crowded.

Sports
There is 18 hole, par 72 golf at Golf Poniente, km16 on the Palma-Andraitx road and lots of tennis at Costa d'en Blanes' Sporting Tenis Playa. The Club

de Ski Naútico on the Son Maties beach, Palma Nova, has won a well-deserved reputation for its waterskiing facilities and the best bet for windsurfing and other water sports is to check out the Puerto Deportivo Palma Nova, the resort's marina.

NORTH MALLORCA

The north of the island is particularly associated with two creative giants: the English poet Robert Graves, who made his home in the village of Deià on the north coast; and Frédéric Chopin, who spent some time in Valldemosa.

Approaches to the North
The round trip from Palma to Valldemosa, Deià and the little town of Sóller involves leaving the capital on the Valldemosa road, travelling from there along the north coast on the C-710 to Deià and to Sóller and returning to Palma from Sóller on the C-711. Distances are very manageable: Valldemosa is 12 miles (19km) from Palma; Deià is about 7½ miles (12km) further on and Sóller, 7 miles (11km) from Deià, is 19 miles (30km) from Palma on the C-711.

There is an alternative to Sóller, and a very pleasant one it is, too. This is to take the narrow gauge train, a very desirable streetcar that is something of a relic, which links Palma with Sóller and its port, Puerto de Sóller. From the port you can take boat rides along the coast, stopping off at whichever cove you choose, to be picked up and return to base later in the day. The *cala* called Sa Calobra, which is one of those on the itinerary, is one of Mallorca's most highly rated coves.

WHAT TO SEE

♦♦♦
DEIÀ ✓

For many people Mallorca is associated with the poet Robert Graves; it was Graves who said, and wrote, *Goodbye to All That* after surviving the World War I trenches, and set up his home on the island. The poet's home was in the village of Deià

A poet's retreat: Deià, beautifully set on a hill among olive groves

on the north coast of the island and it is there, in the village's cemetery with its stunning vistas over the Mediterranean, that he was buried in 1985. If you feel that the magic of Mallorca is taking a grip on you and you want to know why, make the pilgrimage to the north coast to pay homage, in Deià, to Graves' memory.

Just before reaching Deià you pass by **Son Marroig**, the stately mansion which the Archduke Luis Salvador had built for himself. The gardens are exactly what Mediterranean gardens should look and smell like. The Archduke was a 19th-century

Sun and sport in Puerto de Sóller

Austrian aristocrat, who was as enlightened and eccentric as he was charming and wealthy. A genuine lover of the island, he was an ecologist long before his time and bought up large estates with the chief object of protecting the area's natural beauty. The *Archiduque* is a folk hero in Mallorca, remembered and revered far more than he is in the damp land of his Hapsburg relations. He was an above-average amateur botanist, and the panoramic views of the sea from his gardens are sensational. The mansion itself now houses a permanent collection of Mallorcan arts and crafts that includes good furniture and ceramic exhibits (closed Sundays).

It is hard to fault Deià as far as the picturesque is concerned. It is very pretty, and fabulously positioned on high ground surrounded by extensive olive groves and overlooking a gorgeously secluded grove (which inevitably gets crowded in the high season). Serious poets and musicians have taken up residence in Deià and art lovers throng to their exhibitions. But one could quibble that Deià is rather self conscious and has taken the whole Robert Graves temple scenario rather too much to heart.

◆◆◆
SÓLLER
The approaches to this extremely agreeable little town are very lovely, for it is set in a valley of orange groves that is framed by the Sierra de Tramontana range of hills. Sóller's distinguishing feature is that unlike everywhere else in Mallorca, it is a place that has, in a sense, come down a bit in the world. In the last century the town was a thriving textile centre and was sufficiently

important to be linked by railroad to Palma. The textile industry has all but vanished and the railway is now a tourist pleasure trip. Sóller itself is now pleasantly dormant and its port is, naturally, a resort.

Vestiges of a grander past remain in Sóller by way of its Baroque convent church, **Convento de San Francisco**. The 17th-century parish church is worth visiting, as is the town museum, which has a local arts and crafts collection.

Puerto de Sóller, the town's port, is a 3-mile (5km) drive or narrow gauge rail trip down to the coast. This is a perfect little rounded bay, and it boasts an underwater fishing and scuba diving school. Boat trips from here take you along the coast, a stretch of shoreline aptly called Costa Rocosa or Rocky, towards Sa Calobra.

On the C-711 road south to Palma you will pass the **Gardens of Alfàbia** (closed Sundays) some 9 miles (14km) out of Sóller. Anybody who likes gardens, and particularly those that are evocative of a romantic past, should set time aside for a visit.

◆◆◆
VALLDEMOSA ✓

The approach from Palma to this most *bijou* of Mallorca's old villages is along the valley called S'Esglaieta, which offers the picture-postcard island landscape of almond and olive tree groves. Valldemosa itself nestles in the southern folds of the Sierra de

Tramontana and is cosily shielded by them. These hills score their way right across the north of Mallorca and descend abruptly into the sea in the northwest at Cabo Formentor. Valldemosa has a very obvious 18th-century feel about it; this is because the building that has taken place over the last 200 years has on the whole kept to that period's architectural guidelines.

The **Charterhouse** of Valldemosa was home during the winter months of 1838-39 to Frédéric Chopin and his travelling companion of the time, the French novelist George Sand. The Polish composer was consumptively ill that year and the sophisticated Sand felt put out by the situation: the locals disliked her because she smoked and wore trousers, and she cordially loathed them in return for their rustic mentality. In Valldemosa Chopin wrote his gloomy *Funeral March*, which summed up his current feelings about life; and Sand wrote a little book called *A Winter in Mallorca*, in which she took her revenge for her hardships on the island.

Once in the village you will notice how all roads, and all the lines of parked coaches during the high season, lead to La Cartuja, the Charterhouse or Carthusian abbey which was originally the palace of the kings of Mallorca in the 13th century. In 1835 the Charterhouse was privatised and its estates were sold to local landowners. The monks

left and Chopin and George Sand were among the first of the new arrivals. Highpoints of the guided tour of the Charterhouse are a visit to the rooms once used by the abbey's Prior, and to the adjoining rooms, or cells, that were used by Chopin and his lady love. The Prior's suite houses a remarkable library of rare books and an attractive marble triptych from the 15th century; and Chopin's room contains the piano which he used. The Charterhouse's 18th-century pharmacy is also visited. The wise apothecary monk had a legend written up in the store which still stands, and which was obviously his fall-back should his herbal recipes fail to heal a given patient: 'God is the only true Medicine'.
Closed: Sundays

Accommodation

Es Moli (tel: 639000) is a lovely hotel set between Valldemosa and Deià; and so is **La Residencia**, which is inside Deiá on Calle Son Moragues (tel: 639011).

Restaurants

In Valldemosa an unfussy meal of wholesome Mallorcan fare can be had in a nice village house at **C'an Pedro**, which can be found on Avenida Archiduque Luis Salvador.

THE NORTHEAST OF MALLORCA

At its northeasterly point, the island of Mallorca becomes a

The monastery at Valldemosa, where the consumptive composer Frédéric Chopin stayed with his companion George Sand

spindly finger, Cabo
Formentor, that sticks out far
into the Mediterranean. The
cape, which is really a
peninsula, forms a perfect
northern protection to the bays
of Pollença and of Alcudia. The
two bays are themselves
divided by an isthmus which is
where the town of Alcudia is
located.

Do not confuse Alcudia with
Puerto de Alcudia (meaning
'Port of Alcudia') which is the
harbour and resort on the bay
of the same name; nor Pollença,
which is inland, with Puerto de
Pollença, which is likewise on
the bay – the Bahia de Pollença.
In this part of the island you will
come across well developed,
usually upmarket resorts, the
odd quaint village and a lot of
picture postcard views and
sights. The two bays have first
class beaches with clean, white
sand. There is a marshy, sand
dune area on the Bahia de
Alcudia which is excellent for
walks and even better for bird
watching.

The cape/peninsula of
Formentor, with its rocks, pine
trees, towering cliffs and tiny
coves is generally reckoned to
offer the most spectacular
scenery on the island. The road
to its lighthouse is considered a
top attraction for visitors to
Mallorca. The Hotel Formentor
is very luxurious and a historic
landmark as it was the first
specifically 'resort' hotel to be
built on the island, or in the
whole of Spain.

Approaches to the Northeast

If you are based in or around
Palma you can take a day's
round trip drive which will take
in a fair chunk of the island.
From Palma take the N-15 to
Alcudia, a road which passes
through the town of Inca (see
Inland Mallorca, below) at its
halfway point.

When you have seen and done
all you want to do in Puerto de
Alcudia and the Bahia de Alcudia
head north, by way of Alcudia,
on the C-712 to Puerto de
Pollença and from there you can
drive into Cabo Formentor, all
the way to the famed lighthouse.
The return trip goes from
Puerto de Pollença to Pollença
on the C-710 and then on to
Lluc and to Sóller (See **North
Mallorca**, above). At Sóller turn
left onto the C-711, which takes
you back to Palma by way of
Bunyola. A faster alternative is to
turn left at Lluc and drive south
to Inca, where you pick up
the N-15 again and thus take the
return journey to Palma by the
same road on which you left it.

WHAT TO SEE

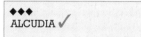

♦♦♦
ALCUDIA ✓

This is the place for a touch of
antiquity and culture. The
village was built near the site of
a 2nd-century Roman settlement
called **Pollentia**. The trophies of
several digs in the area are
exhibited at the **Museo
Arquéologico Municipal**, Calle
San Jaime 2 (closed Mondays)
and the best ruins, among them
recognisable bits and pieces of
a small Roman theatre, are to be
found just outside the village.
Antique relics aside, Alcudia
has 14th-century city walls, two

Cabo Formentor's coastal lookout

very good fortified gates, 17th-century mansions and an attractive parish church dating from the same baroque period and containing good examples of that period's ornately carved altarpieces. The town is a refreshing break from the hi-tech resorts which have no sign of historical interest left at all.

◆◆◆
CABO FORMENTOR ✓

This northern peninsula, 48 miles (78km) from Palma, is one of the island's most fêted beauty spots. Here there are the highest cliffs on the island (the peninsula is a prolongation into the sea of the Tramontana mountain range) and the most dense pine forests. Formentor also boasts Mallorca's clearest waters and its whitest and cleanest beaches – though these claims are disputed by

rival picturesque coves on the island's other shores.

You enter the peninsula along a route from Puerto de Pollença which is as scenic as you could wish. The pine trees, the cliffs and turquoise waters are more and more stunning as you progress into the Cabo.

One favoured stopping place is the **d'es Calomer** lookout, which has magnificent views of the whole rocky coast and of the sea. You will need a good head for heights at this vantage point – you reach it by steps carved into the rock face.

◆◆
POLLENÇA

This town has a pleasing air of culture and refinement about it. Pollença has traditionally been associated with intellectuals and is referred to, somewhat exaggeratedly, as an artists' colony. The **Convent of Santo Domingo** has a museum featuring medieval to modern works of art (closed Tuesdays, Thursdays and Sunday afternoons). The town is indisputably pretty, with narrow little streets and pastel painted cottages in the town centre, and Moorish looking water mills on the outskirts. Peace and tranquillity are readily available for the town is 4 miles (6km) from the coast.

The town is ensconced between two hills. Puig (Mallorcan for Mountain) de Pollença is the higher one and stands 1,000ft (320m) high, while Puig Del Clavari (which means Mount Calvary) is on the west side of town and is much the more intersting of the two.

Puig Del Calvari ✓

The mountain is crowned by an old white-washed chapel which is reached by exactly 365 steps – which visitors invariably count. It is a tiring climb but is, at least, shaded, for the stone steps are flanked by stately cypress trees. On Good Friday religious services are held at the chapel and a torchlit procession winds its way down Puig del Calvari's steps.

◆
PUERTO DE ALCUDIA
A mile (1.6km) away from Alcudia lies Puerto de, or Port of Alcudia on the Bahia de, or Bay of Alcudia. This is the northerly end of a 9-mile (15km) beach, the longest in Mallorca, which

runs right round to the bay's southern point, Cape (or Cabo) Ferrutx. Developments here have made an effort not to wreck the coastline completely. There are several alternative beaches to choose from. You can explore the promontory diving the Pollença and the Alcudia bays. Here there are food coves to scramble down to. This little peninsula is also the site of a 500-year-old shrine, the **Ermita de la Victoria**, which stands at a height of over 1,400ft (444m) on the north of the cape. The views from the Ermita are marvellous. For big, sandy beaches it is also worth trying the resort of **Ca'n Picafort**, which is about halfway between Puerto de Alcudia and the bay's southern point, Cabo Ferrutx. You can reach this tourist centre by following the C-712 south along the Bahia de Alcudia. For a secluded spot which is not a hidden or virtually inaccessible cove, or *Cala*, explore the bird sanctuary area called **La Albufera**, off the C-712 and stretching from Alcudia to La Puebla and Muro. This is a marshy part of the island with sand dunes and pine trees which come down to the sea's edge. With a bit of luck you will have the place to yourself and to the close on 200 bird species which ornithologists say have been spotted in the place.

◆
PUERTO DE POLLENÇA
This used to be Pollença's little harbour, and it is the sort of place about which the 'I was in Mallorca before the tourists' brigade and other bores of that

ilk will wax lyrical, saying they knew Puerto de Pollença when only a couple of fishermen and their barefoot wives and children lived in it. Today it is packed with hotels and apartments. Windsurfng and waterskiing are popular here.

Accommodation

Formentor, Playe de Formentor (tel: 865300) is a very grand hotel indeed. To check on how gracious living is alive and well on Formentor peninsula you should drop in for a drink here. If you want a bed for the night in high season remember that you ought to book now for a room some time next decade: it is that sort of place. The lighthouse is 8 miles (13km) from the hotel. You will find it hard to keep your eyes on the road but make an effort to do so for, as you approach the lighthouse, the sheer drop down to the sea is a good 600ft (200m). Puerto de Alcudia is well served in this direction. The **Princesa**, Avenida Minerva (tel: 892950) is the most expensive and luxurious and the **Condesa de la Bahía**, Urbanización Lago Esperanza (tel: 545324) is huge and more reasonable.

Restaurants

The **Es Segay** on Muro Beach near Puerto de Alcudia is perfect for the fastidious palate.

THE EAST COAST OF MALLORCA

Every string of Mallorca postcards you buy, every brochure of the island that is pushed into your hands will include shots of the caves. Obviously some people will endure anything rather than submit themselves to the confines of underground lakes and forests of stalactites. If you suffer from claustrophobia, skip this section and strike the east coast off your touring agenda.

In their defence, the caves are of the upmarket variety. In no way are they black little holes in the ground. Mallorca, between Cala Ratjada and Porto Colóm on the east coast, boasts really fine, huge caverns. They are a major tourist attraction and as such they are well lit and the tours around them are perfectly organised. A tour of the caves is really a visit to a sci-fi museum (the Artá caves reputedly inspired Jules Verne's *Journey to the Centre of the Earth*). It is certainly not an exercise in pot-holing.

Approaches to the East Coast

To see the caves, you will need to reach either Artá, which is within striking distance of the Artá cave complex, or Manacor, which is the inland town that serves the Dels Hams caves and the Drach caves.

Artá, 39 miles (63km) from Palma, is reached easily enough from Alcudia and Pollença and the northeast resorts by way of the C-712. From Palma and the southwest of the island you approach Artá via Manacor on the C-715. Manacor is a good crossroads reference point for exploring the island. It is linked to the south, to Santanyi and to Felantix, by the C-714, to Palma by the C-715 and to Inca by the inland link road that passes through Petra.

WHAT TO SEE

◆◆◆
THE ARTÁ CAVES

If you want to combine caves with beaches and sightseeing, include the resort of Cala Ratjada, 7 miles (11km) north of the caves, and also the old village of Capdepera, 1½ miles (2.5km) west of Cala Ratjada, in your itinerary (see entries below). The starting point for all three is Artá itself.

The Cuevas de (Caves of) Artá compete with those called del Drach (of the Dragon) further south as the most impressive on the island. Like all such underground complexes on the island's shore, the caves were formed by sea water erosion. The Artá caverns now stand 115ft (35m) above sea level and they delve some 980ft (300m) into the rockface rising, at some points, to a height of 148ft (45m).

The visit takes you through a series of chambers in which the imagination, excited by the suggestive shapes of the stalactites and the stalagmites, is purposefully tuned to Dante: the chambers' names include Hell, Purgatory and Paradise. The caverns served as a hiding place for the Moors fleeing from the Christian invasion of the island and, inevitably, they were also a pirate den.

Just outside Artá is the megalithic village of **Ses**

Pollença's colourful market

Artá, where neolithic stone is still used to build walls

Paisses, while at **Sa Canova** there are neolithic stone remains called *Talayots* (sufficiently common to be used as walls).

CALA RATJADA

Once a fishing village, this is now a well-equipped resort to the north of the Artá Caves, with all the usual facilities. The resort has its own beach and is flanked by a number of coves such as Cala Mesquida, Cala de Sa Font, Cala Aguila and Son Moll.

Away from the beach, the **Casa March Gardens** at Sa Torre Cega, with a notable modern sculpture collection, can be visited by prior arrangement (tel: 563033).

CAPDEPERA

A pleasant little walled village west of Cala Ratjada, with a 13th-century castle. You can drive into it but beware of the very narrow streets and the parking difficulties. It is best to go into the village centre on foot, up a flight of stairs. The lighthouse is worth visiting if only because the exceptional view from it allows you to decide which of the various coves around Cala Ratjada looks best.

♦♦♦
THE DRACH CAVES ✓

The Cuevas del Drach (The Dragon's Caves) are really immense. The complex of caverns stretches for about a mile (1.6km) and it includes a series of underground pools, the biggest of which, called Lake Martel, is all of 580ft (177m) long and is explored by boat. There are enough stalactites and stalagmites and endless strange formations here to last you a lifetime of cavernous reminiscences. You really ought not to feel daunted by these caves should you be worried about claustrophobia. The lighting is extremely clever and civilisation extends sufficiently to allow background music.

Concerts, with music played from boats on Lake Martel, take place several times daily.

If you become hooked on caves, include the nearby **Cuevas dels Hams** in your itinerary. The distinguishing feature of this complex – which was originally an underground river – is that the stalactites are amazingly white and their name, dels Hams, means 'white ceramic tiles'.

◆

SON SERVERA

This town looks out onto the bay of the same name and tourism makes a strong appearance here in the shape of resorts on the bay's **Cala Millor** and **Cala Bona**. Son Servera has a watchtower and a fortified church, sure evidence that pirates were once a constant threat.

The town is close to the **Costa de los Pinos**, one of Mallorca's most exclusive coastal developments. The millionaire villas here, close to and yet sealed off from apartment blocks and hotels, illustrate how fish and chips and caviar and blinis exist (almost) cheek by jowl.

Cala Millor has a pretty strenuous nightlife during the high season for there is no shortage of bars and discos. There is 9-hole golf at the Club de Golf Son Servera, on the

Costa de los Pinos.

Accommodation

The **Hipocampo Playa**, at the quieter end of Cala Millor beach (tel: 585262), and **Sabina Playa**, between Cala Millor and Cala Bona (tel: 585653), are modern, three-star hotels.

Restaurants

Good food in the Son Servera area is available at **Son Floriana**, Urbanización 6, on Cala Bona and the fairly expensive **S'Era de Pula** which is just outside Son Servera on the road to Capdepera.

El Patio, Calle Burdils 45, is a pleasant restaurant in the tourist resort of Porto Cristo, north of the Cuevas dels Hams; the rather more expensive **Ses Comes**, Avenida Pins 24, and **Ca's Patro Pelat**, Carretera del Port 9, are also in Porto Cristo. In Cala Ratjada the **Lorenzo** restaurant, Calle Leonor Servera 11 has a reputation for fish dishes.

THE WEST COAST OF MALLORCA

The west coast of Mallorca provides a bit of everything. There is a chance to stand back from the maddening crowd and wander about inland villages encased in almond groves and tranquillity; there is every opportunity, also, to have the full tourist treatment. Exploring this area does provide the opportunity to grasp the essential contrasts of Mallorca. The island is old, sleepy and timeless but it has, in places, been jerked with a vengeance into the present and into the future. The island is a place which has survived invasions and moulded them into its own culture. Whether it will survive the present package tour invasion and the plundering of the developers is another matter. In this west coast area you can appreciate how, despite all, there are places that have remained more or less untouched, and this can be regarded as a hopeful sign. The village of **Calviá**, as opposed to the resorts lining what is known as the Calviá coast on the Bahia de Palma, is a case in point. Calviá village is, astonishingly, the administrative centre for the noisy strips of neon lights and strobes, discos and junk food bars on the nearby coast.

When you visit its charming little main square and take in the unchanging peace of its green-shuttered houses you are hard put to believe this. This quiet inland town is 6 miles (10km) back from Santa Ponsa. Its main feature is the attractive 13th-century parish church.

Approaches to the West Coast

From Palma, you can reach the port of Andraitx, the furthest point on the west coast and 16 miles (25km) from Palma, by taking the N-13 main road, passing all the Bahia de Palma resorts on your left, and then continuing on the C-719, which takes you through Paguera. To make a round trip of the west coast excursion you could turn

A familiar scene on the Balearic Islands: holiday-makers line up on the beach at Paguera

off the highway at the cross-roads to Palma Nova, taking the right turn to Calviá which lies 4 miles (6km) inland.

The rough idea of the trip is to continue from Calviá to Es Capdella and from there by the same byroads, normally free of traffic, to Andraitx.

Once you have reached your objective you can hit the coast at two points: Puerto de Andraitx, (the port of Andraitx), or San Telmo. Both are tiny harbours and marinas on little custom-built coves and, of course, the two have their share of tourist developments. Boats can be hired from either cove to reach the island of Sa Dragonera. Returning along the coast to Paguera from Andraitx you are on the C-719. A detour back to the sea front before reaching the N-13 highway brings you to Santa Ponsa. An alternative is to drive straight to Paguera from the port of Andraitx along the cliff-top route that passes by yet another little picturesque cove and fishing-cum-resort village, Es Camp de Mar.

WHAT TO SEE

ANDRAITX
This very agreeable valley village comes complete with almond and olive groves and scarcely spoilt popular architecture. In this sense it is in the mould of Calviá and of Capdella, which lies between the two. The village is typical of those built back from the sea in Mallorca in an attempt to escape pirate raids, and the fortified buildings and watchtowers in

this area are an indication of how real the threat of those attacks was right up until the late 18th century.

PUERTO DE ANDRAITX
An alternative side trip from Andraitx. There is plenty of fishing village charm to this place, as well as a lot of pleasure boats and yachts. Other pleasant possibilities centred on Andraitx include hiking trips. There is excellent cliff-top and forest walking along well set out paths around San Telmo and if you go to the nearby hamlet of S'Arraco you will come across an estate called **Sa Trapa**, which used to be the site of a Trappist monastery and which now belongs to the island's Ornithological Society. The coastal road north of Andraitx (C-710) to Estellencs is very scenic.

SA DRAGONERA
Just half a mile (1km) off the coast of San Telmo lies the narrow, rocky island of Sa Dragonera. It is 4 miles (7km) long, has a lighthouse at either end and is shaped like a dragon, if you apply a bit of poetic licence; hence its name. Lighthouse people apart, the only permanent mammals on the island are said to be wild goats, although you will be hard put to see them.

You can reach Sa Dragonera by boat from either Puerto de Andraitx or San Telmo. Once there you are left to your own picnicking devices and you are certain of solitude. For most

Drinks and scenery at Santa Ponsa

people the illusion of having a Mediterranean island of your own is more than enough reason for making the visit. Others go there because it has arguably the best scuba diving possibilities in Mallorca. At night spirits are said to inhabit Sa Dragonera – dragons, and the like.

◆
SANTA PONSA
On the bay of the same name, this is a busy, cosmopolitan resort and that means that it is packed and has nothing particularly Mallorcan about it. It is, nevertheless, a considerable milestone in the island's history, for it was here that the troops of King James I the Conqueror landed in 1229 to take the island from the Moors and for the Christians. Indisputably, Santa Ponsa does have good facilities for fast tans by day and fast fun by night. The beaches are as busy as the discos. Pretty much the same

can be said for the resort of **Paguera**, which is on the north side of the same bay, although this tourist magnet styles itself as slightly more upmarket. Santa Ponsa has very good scuba diving possibilities, as has most of Mallorca, but in particular its west coast. There is 18-hole golf at Golf Santa Ponça I and there is a lot of sailing activity; Santa Ponsa's marina has room for 500 vessels.

Accommodation
The **Club Camp de Mar** is a luxury hotel at Camp de Mar, Puerto de Andraitx (tel: 105200) but there are several hostelries in the area which are slightly more downmarket.

Restaurants
Restaurants abound in Puerto de Andraitx and good eating is assured at **Miramar**, Avenida Mateo Bosch 22, and at **Mola Club**, Urbanización La Mola.

INLAND MALLORCA

Inland Mallorca can be explored on an enjoyable round trip from Palma which will take you on an extended spin through the island and keep you well back from the coast. This is a countryside tour for those who want a break from crystal clear waters and from the stench of sun tan oil. The journey is essentially an inland circle and can be joined at several points. If you are not based in Palma and in the west of the island, you can enter the inland circle at Inca, if you are starting from the north; at Manacor, if you are approaching the tour from the east; and at Felantix or Campos if you are coming from the south.

The tour takes you through towns that give you the other side of Mallorca. Some resorts give the impression that the entire island is given over to the task of keeping mostly non-Spanish holidaymakers fully amused. In point of fact Mallorca does possess, in addition, an agricultural sector that has existed since time immemorial and also a number of industries, the most important of which are shoe manufacturing, glass blowing and the production of artificial pearls.

An exploration of inland Mallorca gives you an insight into an economy that is both more balanced and more mixed than might appear at first sight. Tourism, naturally, accounts for the lion's share of the island's Gross Domestic Product; but life does exist in Mallorca beyond the water-skiing school.

Approaches to Inland Mallorca

The inland circle is formed by the C-713, Palma Inca; the branch road passing through Petra that links Inca-Manacor; the C-714, Manacor-Felantix; the Felantix-Campos branch road and, completing the circle, the C-717, Campos-Palma that passes thorough Llucmayor. The C-715 linking Manacor to Palma, 30 miles (48km), cuts the ring into two neat semicircles and thereby allows you to tour either of them independently.

The Palma-Inca stretch is 17 miles (27km); Inca-Manacor is 19 miles (31km); the Manacor-Felantix stretch of the C-714 is 9 miles (14km); Felantix-Campos is 8 miles (13km), and the C-717 home stretch, Campos-Palma, is 23 miles (37km) of which the last 7 miles (11km) are on the airport freeway.

WHAT TO SEE

◆
CAMPOS

Eight miles (13km) from Felantix (see below) and on the C-717 that leads back to Palma by way of Llucmayor, Campos is worth a stop if you are a pastry and cake enthusiast. This little village is famous for them. It also has some interesting buildings.

Turning left as you reach Campos and the C-717 from Felantix, and heading away from Palma, you will be driving to **Santanyi**, 8 miles (13km), and to the resorts of southeast Mallorca. The coves here range from the almost empty **Cala Santanyi** to the trendy and noisy **Cala d'Or**.

FELANTIX

Linked to Manacor by the C-714 and 30 miles (48km) from Palma, Felantix is an old town dating back to the 13th-century Christian conquest of Mallorca. It is one of the places on the island where you can sample the local wine. Too little wine is produced in Mallorca to make much of it commercially available – which is not altogether a bad thing, for it is pretty rough and polite people say it is an acquired taste. Felantix is currently on the cultural map as the birthplace of **Miquel Barceló**, a contemporary Spanish painter who is as young as he is brilliant and commercially successful. Barceló keeps a studio in his home town but you will have to go to New York's Greenwich Village galleries if you want to buy his arresting, giant canvasses. From Felantix you can head 7 miles (12km) southeast to the coast and to the **Porto Colóm** fishing village (mostly unspoilt) and resort (mostly tasteful). On the way to the coast you can turn left and follow the road up to a 1,600ft (500m) rise where the **Monasterio San Salvador** stands. This is a medieval monastery whose church is graced with a very fine Gothic altarpiece. Other reasons for this 4 mile (7km) detour are the extremely good views and

the chance to sample nourishing local fare, rice and the rest, at an inn just by the monastery.

INCA

This town has the distinction of having the most popular weekly market on the island, as well as the oldest one; there are 13th-century records of merchants bringing their produce to fairs held at Inca. The market is held every Thursday, and that would be a sensible day to visit the town. Nowadays Inca is one of the most important centres of Mallorca's leather and footwear industry. Don't expect to find large factories, though; shoes, at least here, are manufactured, or rather assembled, in small workshops.

Inca has little of architectural note about it; but the **Iglesia** (Church) **de Santa Maria la Mayor** has the best bell tower you are likely to find anywhere on the island; and the **Conventos** (Convents) **de Santo Domingo** and **de San Francisco** have unexpectedly appealing cloisters. All three buildings are essentially baroque in style and in intent, although there are parts of the Santa Maria Church that go right back to the 13th century, when the first stones were laid. The town also produces biscuits, *ensaimada* – large, flaky pastries usually eaten for breakfast and tea, and sometimes stuffed with spicy sausage or custard or candied fruit; and a type of cake called *cocac*, versatile pizza-style pies which can be topped with vegetables, anchovies, or custard and fruit. If you want to buy the genuine article, or at least to make a story out of your purchase, acquire them directly from **Convento de las Jerónimas**, where the nuns make them.

North of the town, on the road to Lluc, a 3-mile (4.5km) drive will bring you to the pleasant little old village of **Selva**, which boasts a rather good Gothic church, the **Iglesia de San Lorenzo**, which is scenically framed by cypress trees. A Calvary altarpiece inside the church is, in its shocking realism, a typical example of Spanish religious sculpting. If you carry on towards Lluc you will pass by the **Selva** itself – it means sacred forest in Mallorcan – and the **Monasterio**

Porto Colóm fishing village

(Monastery), or **Santuario** (Sanctuary) **de Lluc** where a statue of the Virgin is revered as the spiritual patron of the island.

Back at Inca, the Puig (Mallorcan for mountain peak) de Inca looms over the town and you can drive 2½ miles (4km) up to the top and visit the **Santuario Santa Magdalena** for a good view of the centre of the island: the so-called Pla (Plain) de Mallorca.

◆
LLUCMAYOR
A solid manufacturing town, mostly shoes, Llucmayor has its tourist side to it, for it is the administrative centre for the beaches on the eastern side of the Bahia de Palma.

The beaches and the cliffs from **Cabo Enderrocat** down south to **Cabo Blanco** are unusually empty, sufficiently so to be popular among birdwatchers. A

2½-mile (4km) detour north from Llucmayor takes you up into the hills for great views of Palma and its bay. Follow the road to the **Monasterio del Cura**, a monastery that is associated with the talented medieval traveller and scholastic **Ramón Llul** (see **Palma**, above). He is said to have tended a herb garden in this monastery and he certainly spent some time reading here, for some of his manuscripts survive in the monastery's library.

MANACOR

Together with Inca and Llucmayor, this is one of the island's year-round population centres and, like them, it is a fair-sized manufacturing centre. Manacor has an important furniture-making industry, but its real claim to fame is that it is the home of the cultured, or artificial pearl. If you wear fake pearls you should drop in on Manacor's **Perlas Majórica** factory at Vía Roma 52. Again like Inca, Manacor is on the whole characterless, but it does have its distinctive points. The Archaeological Museum, **Museo Arqueológica Municipal**, is strong on mosaics and Stone Age remains as well as ceramics, and there is a fortification called the **Torre** (Tower) **des Enagistes**, which is the last vestige of what was the summer residence used by the 13th-century conqueror of Mallorca, James II. The **Iglesia de San Vicente**, 17th century,

has a very good cloister. Manacor is the administrative centre for nearby coastal resorts such as **Porto Cristo** and for the popular caverns of the **Cuevas del Drach** (see **East Mallorca**).

PETRA

This village, northwest of Manacor, is the birthplace of **Fray Junípero de la Serra**, the tireless evangelist who opened missions in California with an incredible determination. There is a statue to the enterprising Friar here, and also a museum, the **Museo Junípero Serra**, which is the very house where he was born. It has 18th-century bric-à-brac and souvenirs, Junípero's convent, the **Convento de San Bernardino**, is also open to the public and, as you might suppose, there are statues in the church dedicated to San Francisco, to San Diego and to Santa Bárbara, the saints after whom he named missions that were later to become big cities.

Accommodation

The **Ermita de Neustra Senora de Bon Any**, on a hilltop southwest of Petra offers good, simple lodgings (tel: 561101).

Restaurants

Inca has a particularly good selection of wholesome local food restaurants, as befitting any self-respecting market town. Many are located in old wine cellars dating from the time when Mallorca produced its own vintages. **Cellar Ca'n Amer**, Calle Bruy 7, is a typical example of such hostelries.

Though Menorca's tourist crowds are growing, some quiet beaches remain

MENORCA

Menorca, although it styles itself the second largest of the Balearic Islands, is only slightly larger than Ibiza and is a third of the size of Mallorca. It runs for 30 miles (48km) and for 12 miles (19km) at its longest and widest points. The essential difference from its sister isles is that it is less developed as a tourist resort, and the island's authorities did, in fact, try to shield Menorca from mass arrivals of visitors. A more discriminating tourist was preferred.

The attempts to keep Menorca 'quainter' and less touristy were doomed from the start, for the island has undeniable attractions. The scenery is remarkably green inland, even at the height of summer, and it was only a matter of time before people caught on to what were by common consent some of the loveliest, as well as the least crowded, beaches in the Balearics. Menorca's development gap with Mallorca and with Ibiza is inexorably closing.

The Layout

The island is essentially flat but it is varied nonetheless. The north coast, more rocky and rugged, as is the norm in each of the Balearic Islands, is exposed to the Tramontana winds. There are wide valleys here and Aleppo pine, wild olive and fig trees abound. The north coast is the most verdant part of the island while the best beaches, a succession of picturesque little coves with superbly clear waters, are in Menorca's southeast corner within striking distance of Mahón. The south coast, well protected from the Tramontana winds, is one long cliff, peppered every so often with small inlets and their accompanying solitary beaches.

The main axis of the island is the east-west road which runs along its middle, linking the two main port towns of Mahón and Ciudadela. This takes you through the small inland towns, from east to west, of Alayor, Mercadal and Ferrerías.

These are agricultural centres with attractively whitewashed cottages and roads lead off them both to the north and the south, towards the beach resorts.

Ancient History

Menorca may be the least developed of the Balearics nowadays but there is undisputable evidence that it was inhabited by an energetic population long before any of the other islands. A booming Bronze Age civilisation left fairly hefty footprints behind it in the form of *Taulas,* T-shaped formations of stone which are unique to Menorca, and in *Talayots* – larger, conical-shaped piles of rocks.

The prehistoric Taula de Trepucó at Es Castell (see page 56)

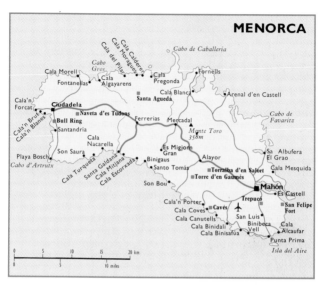

MENORCA

Cabo de Caballeria
Cala Morell
Cabo Gros
Cala del Pilar
Cala Calderer
Cala Moragues
Fontanellas
Cala Algayarens
Cala Pregonda
Fornells
Cala'n Forcat
Cala Blanca
Arenal d'en Castell
Ciudadela
Santa Agueda
Cala'n Brut
Cala'n Blanes
Naveta d'es Tudons
Bull Ring
Santandria
Ferrerias
Mercadal
Cabo de Favaritx
Son Saura
Cala Nacarella
Monte Toro 358m
Es Migjorn Gran
Sa Albufera El Grao
Playa Bosch
Cabo d'Artrutx
Cala Turqueta
Santa Galdana
Cala Mitjana
Binigaus
Alayor
Cala Mesquida
Cala Escorxada
Santo Tomás
Torralba d'en Salort
Torre d'en Gaumés
Son Bou
Mahón
Es Castell
Trepucó
Cala'n Porter
Cala Coves
Cavés
San Felipe Fort
Cala Canutells
San Luis
Cala Binidali
Binibeca Vell
Cala Binisafúa
Cala Alcaufar
Punta Prima
Isla del Aire

0   5   10   15   20 km
0   5   10 miles

There is no real consensus as to what these remains represent. The larger *Talayots*, of which there are hundreds, could have served as watchtowers and the eight *Taulas* might have been demarcation points among tribes and could have doubled as religious centres. Proper archaeological research in the south of the island still awaits sponsors and professionals. Menorca received visits from Phoenicians, Greeks and, finally, Carthaginians and Romans.

The Moors established themselves on the island in the 8th century, when successive Islamic waves occupied the whole of Spain, and Menorca was eventually reclaimed by the Christian rulers of the peninsula at the end of the 13th century.

The British Connection
One of the distinguishing features about Menorca is its association with Britain in the 18th century. The island passed into British hands, as did Gibraltar, as part of the Treaty of Utrecht settlement that put an end, in 1713, to the War of Spanish Succession. In 1802 the island, but not Gibraltar, was returned to Spain. The British Fleet under Admiral Lord Collingwood remained in Mahón, to defend the island against Napoleon, until 1810. Menorca's near century-long British connection left its mark in several different ways. It is most obvious in the old town of Es Castell, 2½ miles (4km) southeast of Mahón, which was the one time British garrison post of Georgetown. The barrack square, the colonial-style town hall and the

Georgian nuances in the local architecture are sure signs of the connection.

The local manufacture of Menorcan gin – it is pretty rough but visitors are honour-bound to try it – is a British legacy and words such as *kitel* for kettle and *bericks* for barracks have become absorbed into the Menorcan language. *Menorquin*, the local dialect, is a bastardised Catalan, as are the dialects spoken on Mallorca and Ibiza. Royal Navy links were established by men such as Admiral Lord Collingwood, who commanded a British Fleet here in the early 19th century. His former residence, on the outskirts of Mahón, is now a charming hotel.

The most famous Briton, as far as Menorca is concerned, was Richard Kane, who had the first road built between Mahón and Ciudadela, and who introduced English livestock and produce onto the island. British occupancy of the island during the 18th century was hotly disputed by the French, who managed to set down beachheads during the period, notably at San Luis. San Luis, just south of Mahón, has an altogether French feel to it and a church that bears the coat of arms of Louis XV.

The Island Economy

Menorca has a well-developed shoe and leather goods sector that is, interestingly, based on a myriad of small manufacturers and suppliers in an extensive cottage industry network. Ciudadela, in particular, is full of tiny one-man shoe factories. Lately, costume jewellery has been gaining ground. Menorca, and specifically Mahón, claims to have invented what Spaniards call *mahonesa* and what the world knows as mayonnaise. This accolade is disputed. The island does, however, have an established culinary brand name in its Mahón cheese, a well cured product.

Tourism is, nevertheless, making steady inroads into the industrial and the agricultural sectors. Many resent this. It is said among Menorcan *aficionados* that, should you find, at the end of a seemingly impassable track, an isolated little beach where the pine trees meet the sand and the sand melts into the crystal waters – you should keep the secret to yourself.

MAHÓN

Menorca's capital, with a permanent population of just over 22,000, is pleasingly unpretentious. There are several buildings of interest, such as the church of **Santa Maria**, which houses one of the finest organs in Europe, and the **Theatre Principal**, a replica of La Scala in Milan, and now also a cinema. Mahón's charm lies in its picturesque collection of whitewashed houses, crowded together along narrow little streets. The style could not be more mixed, for here there are clear Muslim influences and

Bright new holiday facilities meet old Mahón's subdued elegance

strong Georgian influences – the latter being the legacy of British occupancy of Menorca during the 18th century. Yet it is all attractively in harmony. It was the British who moved the island's capital from Ciudadela to Mahón and it is easy to see why. The town's real pride and joy is its natural harbour, which must be one of the best in the world. It was the perfect accommodation for an entire Mediterranean fleet – something that Nelson understood immediately, as did other great seamen such as Barbarossa, who was responsible for a revenge raid on the town during the 16th century.

Well equipped with restaurants and shopping zones, Mahón is within striking distance of good beaches and boasts a number of additional amenities such as a race track, a golf course and a lively yacht club. Compared with the other Balearic capitals, Mallorca's Palma and Ibiza's Eivissa, Mahón scores as a quieter place, less anxious to shout out its attractions from the rooftops. The town's agreeably low profile has something to do with the fact that Mahón is not wholly dependent on tourists: it gets by nicely with the manufacture of down-to-earth products such as cheese. The flavours range from a tender, bland cheese to matured, salty cheeses reminiscent of parmesan.

For a rest from the sun, sand and sangria you could visit the Stone Age remains at **Trepucó**, just outside the town, and if you are not into scuba diving there is always the town's **aquarium**.

WHAT TO SEE

SAN LUIS

Set to the south of Mahón, this village was founded by the French, who vied with the British for the island for much of the 18th century. It has a very French-looking church and an altogether Gallic feel to it. Claims that it is a *bijou* hamlet are not misplaced.

San Luis is also the centre for a number of coastal developments, of which the Binibeca resort area is arguably the most tasteful. Alcaufar is a cove in the area that is worth visiting.

ES CASTELL

This is the old site of the British garrison, to the southeast of Mahón. Once known as Georgetown, after George III, it is English in the manner that San Luis is French. Dominated by the old San Felipe fort, which was built in the 16th century to fire grapeshot at marauding pirates, Es Castell has a particularly scenic

Fishermen's storehouses have become bars in Es Castell harbour

harbour where the old storehouses that used to house fishermen's nets have now been converted into bars.

Beaches
One choice is to head north in the direction of Arenal d'en Castell. However, there are good facilities closer to the town at Cala Mesquida and Sa Albufera El Grao.
There are alternatives heading south, such as the small beaches of **Cala Canutells** and **Cala Binidali**. Many Menorcan-based people head for **Cala'n Porter**, which tends to be overcrowded.

Accommodation
Accommodation in Mahón includes the four-star **Port Mahón**, Avenida Fort de l'Eau, (tel: 362600), in the port area (open during summer only); and the central **Capri**, San Esteban 8 (tel: 361400). Es Castell has four three-star establishments: the largest, **Hamilton**, Paseo de Santa Agueda 6 (tel: 362050) is the only one open all year. Just outside the village of San Luis, the three-star **Biniali**, Suestra 50, on the road to Binibeca Vell beach (tel: 151724), ensures quietly pleasant accommodation.

Nightlife
Mahón's evergreen drinks rendezvous is the **American Bar**, Plaza Real 8, and night-time revelling takes place at two out-of-town venues, **Tonic**, Avenida de Son Vilar, Urbanización Horizonte, Es Castell, a remarkable place, for it is really a cave; and **Lui**, Plaza de Abu Omar, Sa Sinia, which is on the way to Es Castell.

Restaurants
The most picturesque and expensive restaurant, with its grand views of the port, is **Rocamar**, Calle Fonduco 32. **Pilar**, Calle Forn 61 is regarded as serving the most classical local dishes. These include the *caldereta de langosta*, making liberal use of local herbs such as thyme and rosemary, in a lobster stew. Menorca, in common with the other Balearic Islands, produces excellent fish and seafood stews called *caldereta de peix*; the ingredients vary according to the catch. **Gregal**, Moll de Llevant 43 and the **Club Maritimo**, at number 27 on the same street, are good fish restaurants.
All these hostelries are in the moderate to high price range and take all major credit cards.

Shopping
There are many shopping possibilities in Mahón, but connoisseurs frequent places such as **Patricia**, Calle Ses Moreres 31, for shoes and leather goods and **Catisa**, Calle San Sebastian 75, for costume jewellery. A market is held in Explanada Square every Tuesday and Saturday.

Sports
Sports facilities range from sailing to scuba diving (for information check with the Mahón and with the Es Castell yacht clubs) and from golf to

trotting races. There is a 9-hole golf course at the Golf Son Park. Trotting races, to which Menorcans are much addicted, are staged at the Hipodromo, the town's race track. Go-Karting is available at the Aero Club.

CIUDADELA ✓

Menorca's second town, only slightly smaller than Mahón, Ciudadela is the capital of the western end of the island. Whitewashed and Moorish-looking, the town lacks the cosmopolitan shine of Mahón – it is still smarting from the fact that the British turned its rival into Menorca's capital – and is altogether more Spanish.

It is a very old town, which boasted its own bishop in the 4th century long before the Moors arrived and made it their main settlement on the island. Pirate raids caused strong defences to be built, including a wall encircling the town, constructed in the period that followed the Christian reconquest of Menorca from the Moors.

There are traces of former grandeur in the odd Renaissance building in the town centre, as well as in the Gothic **cathedral**, a building which unfortunately had a neo-classical façade added to the original structure.

The town is particularly proud of its network of small shoe-producing workshops, and the footwear industry has long been the main ingredient of its economy. Its harbour, although

far smaller than Mahón's, is a busy place and specialises in lobster fishing.

A visit is worthwhile to the Bronze Age tomb known locally as a *Naveta*, at **Es Tudons**, and the cave drawings of **Santa Ana de Tourraulbet**, close to the Nacarella cove south of the town.

Ciudadela's big claim to fame is the manner in which it celebrates the feast day of St John on 24 June. The heroes of the festivities are daredevil riders and magnificent horses, and the fiesta consists of complex and hair-raising jousting competitions. The events have justifiably been called the equestrian equivalent of the well-known

bullrunning festival of
Pamplona on mainland Spain,
and they are likewise
accompanied by lots of
general drinking and
merrymaking. This celebration
is far and away the best and the
most colourful fiesta to be
found in the whole of the
Balearics.

WHAT TO SEE

Beaches
Ciudadela's local beaches, the
calas or coves of **Blanes**, **Brut**
and **En Forcat**, are the best
equipped and the most
crowded. There are sandy

*Ciudadela is Menorca's second
town, but the imposing town hall
hints at a long and proud past*

beaches south of the town at
Turqueta, **Macarella** and **Son
Saura**, while driving north you
will come across rockier inlets
such as **Alagayarens**,
Fontanellas and **Morell**.

Accommodation
Accommodation in and near
Ciudadela ranges from the
large sea-front **Almirante
Farragut** (tel: 382800), in the
En Forcat Cove, to the **Cala
Blanca** (tel: 380450), also
outside Ciudadela in the
resort development of the
same name; and to the
centrally located **Esmeralda**,
Paseo San Nicolás 171,
(tel: 380250) and the **Patricia**,
Paseo San Nicholás 90–2
(tel: 385511) which is open
all year. All of these hotels
are three-star.

Nightlife
In Ciudadela locals
congregate at the bars on or
around the central Plaza
Alfonso III such as **Ca's
Quintu**, which is the most
traditional of the bunch.
Addagio's, Calle San Oleo, is
the town's only disco.

Restaurants
Casa Manolo, Calle Marina
103 is an establishment
which is famed for its
seafood; Ciudadela's best
restaurant.

Sports
For information about sailing
and underwater fishing you
should approach the Club
Náutico, Ciudadela's yacht
club, and for a day at the
trotting races watch out for
scheduled events at the local
Hipodromo.

THE NORTH AND SOUTH COASTS OF MENORCA

The northern section of Menorca consists of wooded countryside with wide valleys, that gives on to an indented stretch of coast which has so far proved too rocky and exposed to the winds to merit development. The protected southern section of the island is much more urbanised. The coastline here is one long cliff punctuated with scenic coves; most of these have been promoted as tourist resorts.

WHAT TO SEE

ALAYOR

Seven miles (12km) out of Mahón, this is the first of the inland towns you come across on the main east-west road to Cuidadela. Alayor's balconied town houses lend a distinctive 18th-century air to what is basically a self-contained little community that maintains its agricultural and its shoe manufacturing traditions. Alayor's action is to be found by following the signs southwest to the beaches, and in particular to the **Son Bou** resort, 5 miles (8.5km) away. Discriminating visitors should explore the beaches between the resorts of Son Bou and **Es Canutells**. There are a number of little coves approachable along dirt tracks which can be virtually deserted. If you are going off to explore, pack a picnic to cover all eventualities.

There are interesting troglodyte cave dwellings at **Cala Coves** and also in the cliffs by the narrow estuary of **Cala'n Porter**, and very good megalithic remains at **Torralba d'en Salort** and **Torre d'en Gaumés**. Just out of Son Bou there is a ruined Christian shrine, reckoned to date from the 4th century.

FERRERÍAS

Ten miles (16km) from Ciudadela and 5 miles (8km) from Mercadal (see below), Ferrerías is a centre for reproduction Sheraton, Chippendale and Queen Anne-style furniture, dating from the days of British occupation, when island carpenters would copy the master patterns. Ferrerías is also one of the island's shoe making and costume jewellery manufacturing centres. Both cottage industries have made inroads into the village's traditional agricultural economy, and they, in turn, are now rivalled by the expanding tourist interests centred in the Santa Galdana resort, 4 miles (7km) south of Ferrerías. The historically minded should make the effort to see the ruins of the Arab castle of **Sent Agayz**, which was strategically built on the nearby hill called Santa Agueda. There is a cluster of prehistoric remains in the area, such as **Benimassó**, **Binicosstitx**, **Santa Ponsa** and **Son Bell Llot**, which should draw the amateur archaeologist. Hikers should not miss out on the walk along the **Algendar ravine** between Ferrerías and Santa Galdana. North of Ferrerías there are coves east and west of the cape of **Cabo Gros**. The rule of thumb is to drive along a dirt track and walk when the going gets more difficult. There is better access to the beaches called **Calderer**, **Moragues** and **Pilar**, despite which, facilities are few and isolation is virtually assured.

Santa Galdana, mixing good sand, superb waters and pine trees, is one of the finest of the south coast beaches. If you knew it as it once was, and it

The coastline at Santa Galdana beach, once deserted, now caters for the tourist trade

was complete paradise, it is ruined; but if you didn't you won't grieve unduly, and you might enjoy the resort hype and the nightlife. Alternatives are the **Mitjana** and the **Trebelútger** inlets.

♦♦
MERCADAL

In the very centre of Menorca, 14 miles (22km) from Mahón and 15 miles (24km) from Ciudadela, Mercadal lies in a valley at the foot of the 1,171ft (357m) Monte Toro, the highest point of the island. There is a shrine at the summit and from it you can see the entire island. Distinguished by its popular architecture, Mercadal was founded in the Middle Ages.

The village is a useful base from which to explore a selection of beaches on the north and on the south coasts of the island.

Northern Beaches

Most motorists arriving at Mercadal from Mahón take a left turn north at the village on to the C-723 and follow the signs to **Fornells**, 5 miles (8km) away. This is a picturesque little village on the bay, really a fjord, of the same name, where lobster catching has been a main source of income for generations. Fornells' attractions include two sandy coves, **Cala Rotja** and **Cala Blanca**, which have sea sport facilities; a marine cave called **Na Polida** which is well equipped with stalactites and stalagmites; and a good lobster stew restaurant called **Es Plá**. There are also *tapas* bars, notably one called **La Palma**, and shops dealing in leather work.

Those who seek solitude on the beaches should take the dirt tracks northwest of Fornells towards **Cala Pregonda**. An alternative is to head eastwards towards the very fine beach of **Arenal d'en Castell**, which has lately become very popular and is linked by a local road direct to Mahón.

Southern Beaches

Escorxada and **Binigaus** are typical, mostly unspoilt, southern beaches within striking distance of Mercadal. The resort area is the beach of **Santo Tomás**, which has a housing development and hotel facilities that include the four-star Santo Tomás and the three-star Sol Cóndores.

The hamlet of **San Cristóbal**, south of Mercadal, is worth a brief halt because it is held to be the best example of the local architecture. Look out for the open air kitchens, the bread ovens and the rain water collecting systems. Nearby there is a *Talayot* fortified dwelling to be seen in the very old village of **San Agustí**.

Accommodation

The large **Sol Milanos** hotel (tel: 371175) is the epicentre of the Son Bou resort, as is the equally large **Royal Son Bou** (tel: 372358), a hotel-apartment complex boasting a swimming pool, tennis courts and gym.

Nightlife

The **Sa Cova d'en Xoroi** discotheque is very popular with young tourists, and is set in a cave at Cala'n Porter.

Restaurants

Mercadal is worth a visit at mealtimes, as it pays due care and attention to local Menorcan cuisine and also serves *Caldereta de Langosta* – lobster stew.

Particularly recommended are **C'an Naguedet**, Calle Lepanto 30; and **Es Moli d'es Reco**, Es Reco 53. Both are moderate to expensive establishments which accept most credit cards. The **Es Plá** restaurant in Fornells (see above) also serves good lobster stew. Fine Menorcan cuisine can also be sampled at **Hostal Jeni**, Miranda del Toro 81, Mercadel.

IBIZA

Ibiza is really very small indeed. The whole island is only 221 square miles (572sq km), and the C-733 linking Ibiza town with Cala Portinatx on the northern tip of the island, is all of 18 miles (29km) long. The 'small is beautiful' dictum can certainly apply to Ibiza, which can be appealing and attractive. That north to south road will take you through groves of gnarled and knotty olive trees and past gleaming white cottages which have been whitewashed, year in and year out, for as long as the ancient olive trees have been bearing fruit; the cottages, as a result, encased in their layers of whitewash, look as if they have had meringue plastered all over them. Shimmering little farmhouses lie back from the sea, and the delights of rural Ibiza form one image of the island which those in the coastline resorts can miss altogether.

There is also a coastal arcadia for visitors prepared to look for the island's hidden secret coves; these can be reached more easily by sea, but can be approached by land as well, if you are willing to hike and to scale down cliffs.

An essential point to remember about Ibiza is that is does not have to be crowded beaches and sidewalks; but Ibiza can mean multitudes, and of course people do go to the island

Bright whitewashed cottages standout against Ibiza's blue skies

precisely because it does have such popular resorts. This is the other side of the coin to the rural island and its solitary coves, representing package tour Ibiza in resorts such as San Antonio. The latter, 'San Ant' as young Britons call it, offers fast food and discos and holiday frolics for tens of thousands of north European under-25s.

Yet another facet of the island is its appeal to outrageous, pace-setting 'trendies'. One of their base camps is Eivissa (Ibiza town) where many of them deliberately cultivate a sophisticated, unconventional image.

Islands Apart

In its mix of what is remarkably unspoilt and what is little more than a concrete jungle, of what is unchanging and what is constantly moving, Ibiza is very typically part of the Balearics. But though similar, in that respect, to its sister isles, Ibiza is nevertheless very different from Mallorca and Menorca. Together with its satellite island of Formentera, Ibiza belongs to the Pitiusas, or pine-covered isles, and is not technically part of the Balearics at all.

The Pitiusas are the westernmost and the southernmost islands, and they are drier, hotter and flatter. You will notice immediately that Ibiza has a North African air to it, and it owes this as much to the heat-searing African winds that blow over it as it does to the style of the popular architecture. The island is, in fact, closer as the crow and seagull fly, to Algiers than to Barcelona.

There is a historical basis to such impressions: Ibiza was never colonised by the Romans as Mallorca and Menorca were, and Arab civilisation set down stronger roots and lasted longer in Ibiza than elsewhere in the Balearics. All this goes to reinforce the view that Ibiza is a very special and unique place.

Climate, geography and architecture are other elements in Ibiza's uniqueness. But without a doubt the most definitive of Ibiza's characteristics is its uninhibited atmosphere. The 'behave as you please' approach to life applies as much to the young package tour holidaymakers who invade San Antonio in summer as it does to the cosmopolitan crowds of Ibiza town.

Ibiza is a tolerant place, well used to eccentricities. But it can be every bit as outrageous as it can be gentle. There was a time when colonies or families of 'hippies' set up home on the island. Nowadays there is still a good selection of drop-outs of the better-heeled sort. Then, as now, Ibiza stood for doing your own thing in your own way and in your own time. One of the most astonishing features of Ibiza is the manner in which local farmers, fishermen and artisans can ply their trade oblivious to and untouched by the surrounding hustle of high pressure people.

At one level people in Ibiza set the trends of fashion and

A view across the harbour of Eivissa, Ibiza's capital, from the Dalt Villa, or old town

behaviour which are imitated elsewhere in the world two or three seasons later. At another level, of olive groves, of whitewashed cottages and of hidden coves, Ibiza remains utterly impervious to time.

EIVISSA

You may be spending your holidays at any one of a score of resorts on the island, but sooner or later you should set aside a day to visit the island's capital – Ibiza town, or Eivissa. The town's pull is irresistible. It is the sort of place you read about in magazines. If nothing else, Eivissa is a celebrity spot. People go to the island's

capital simply so that they can claim to have been to this exciting place.

Eivissa is, in any case, the natural entry point to the island. You will, of course, be passing through it as you arrive at and as you leave from Ibiza's welcoming airport. If you arrive at Ibiza by boat you will be docking in the town's harbour.

The first fact which needs to be known about Eivissa is that, for the purposes of the visitor and tourist, it is neatly divided into two. There is the Dalt Villa, which is the old town, perched up on the hill; and there is La Marina, the harbour area. The second point worth keeping in mind is that this is a walkers' town. If you do not already possess them, buy your rope-soled sandals, or *espadrilles*, here.

Ideally anyone visiting the town should be taking a rest from the beaches and taking a day to wander around Eivissa. Otherwise the alternatives are to arrive early and return to home base after a fine lunch, or to come in the afternoon fully prepared to see what there is to see and then to follow the crowds into the night spots, which will keep you up long after dawn has broken over the Mediterranean.

To do justice to Eivissa you will want to divide your time between the harbour area, La Marina, and the upper old town, Dalt Vila. Visiting one and not the other amounts to not having been there at all. In theory, and if you hurry, you can do it in half a day. Everyone will have their own list of priorities when it comes to what to do in Ibiza town; every taste is catered for. A rule of thumb is that what is happening, what is worn and what is enjoyable this year in Ibiza will set the form for the rest of Europe the following year. Ibiza has a well-deserved pace-setting reputation. Anyone arriving in the town should be prepared to leave preconceptions and prejudices behind them.

The commonest pastime in Eivissa is 'people watching'. Ibiza is a terrific place for extroverts and those who are not hard at work preening themselves are fully occupied watching the ones who do. There are a number of celebrities, actors, rock people and the like who use Ibiza fairly regularly, but in general the media stars seem to melt into the background when they are surrounded by so many beautiful and extravagant poseurs.

It should be said that people 'dress up' in Ibiza. There is no need to follow suit, but you should know that, for instance, the attractive lady walking down an Eivissa street could turn out to be a man.

A second high priority is shopping (see below). Eivissa has its full share of souvenir emporia and there are many stores dealing specifically with

Shopping and strolling can be entertainment enough in Eivissa

Mediterranean holiday props such as goggles and snorkels, eyeshades and beach mattresses. The nightlife here is also worth sampling. For many, a visit to Ibiza town means stopping by the bars and cafés, moving on to dinner at the right places and ending up in the fashionable discos. Eivissa has as many drinking establishments, eateries and dance palaces as most normal people expect to encounter in a lifetime.

In a different vein, a cultural tour of the Dalt Villa will focus on the old quarter's archaeological museum. If you want to know all about Ibiza's origins and to gain insights into the past of the western end of the Mediterranean, there is little to beat the old quarter's museum.

Approaches to Eivissa

On an island the size of Ibiza, you will quickly find that all roads lead to its main town. You may encounter difficulties trying to reach other places, but you will always know by the milestones on the island's main roads just how far you are from Eivissa. It will never be more than a quick trip.

If you have driven to Ibiza town from Portinatx and the north, leave your car by the outer port, before you reach La Marina. The same applies if you are driving in from San Antonio and from San José: park in the modern part of the town by the broad Avenida de España boulevard or by the Paseo Vara del Rey before approaching the harbour and the old Dalt Villa quarter. Remember, always, to leave nothing (cameras, suitcases, cassette radios, etc) in the car. Even if a parking attendant has issued you with a 25 peseta ticket for the privilege of parking your car in a given area, you should not feel safe about your car-bound possessions. The attendant is not legally responsible for your goods, and if you leave them in full view of potential thieves the official opinion is that you have only yourself to blame for any losses which might occur.

For insurance purposes, report thefts to the local police station – *La Comisaría de Policía* – where an officer will take down the details.

Eivissa's old, steep streets

WHAT TO SEE

♦♦♦
DALT VILLA

The old town, as you climb the hill to enter it, rises above the hustle and the pockets of squalor. If you are searching for the sound of silence in Ibiza town you are more likely to find it here than anywhere else. The Dalt Villa creates a lasting impression on its visitors because it takes on the appearance of a shared secret among foreigners and Spaniards alike.

A visit to this quarter involves clambering uphill through quaint and narrow lanes; penetrating defensive walls; passing the odd substantial town mansion, built by Eivissa's rich and powerful residents; and, every so often, entering a little square or discovering an amazing view of the sea from some pleasant vantage point. The hill was first populated by the Carthaginians in about 700BC and remains from that epoch and from later antique periods are housed in the Dalt Villa's Archaeological Museum and in the nearby Archaeological Museum of Puig des Molins, which has fascinating displays (see below).

Perhaps the most impressive of the surviving historical landmarks is the defensive wall which was built round about the time of the Spanish Armada in the 16th-century reign of Philip II.

The best way to enter the old upper town is through the

superb gateway, set in the walled system, that is called the **Portal de las Tablas**. It has Philip II's coat of arms on it and is decorated with Roman figurines which, at one time, fairly littered the island. The gate leads into the Plaza de la Villa.

There is no chance of getting lost on the Dalt Villa, however labyrinthine its streets might appear to be. The general layout is quite straightforward. If you go uphill you will eventually get to the cathedral and going downhill you will inevitably end up in the Plaza de la Villa and Portal de las Tablas.

As you ascend the hill, you will find that the sea is invariably on your left.

To get the feel of the place the best course is, probably, to go left at the square and wander over to the **Baluarte de Santa Lucía** watchtower, which looks out directly to the sea. From there, continue up to reach the **Plaza de España**, graced with a 17th-century monastery

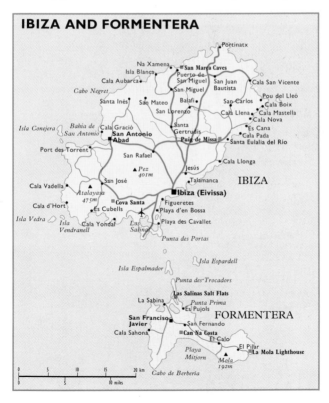

IBIZA AND FORMENTERA

which now houses the Town Hall. The Plaza de España is a Dalt Villa landmark, not so much because of the municipal building, but rather because it is the location of an extremely popular *chiringuito* (a terrace bar), which stays open more or less 24 hours a day. Again, the view of the sea, one of the Dalt Villa's main characteristics, is stunning from this point.
To continue the exploration you could now move inland, as it were, from the Plaza de España along the Calle Pedro Tur which will take you past a couple of fine mansion style houses built in the 18th century; one, called **Casa Riquer**, was the home of Ibiza's most famous pirate, Antonio Riquer, and stands as a testimony to his highly successful career of sharking and plundering, 200 years ago. Just up from the Calle Pedro Tur, on the Calle de Poniente, you will come across **El Corsario**, an extremely pleasant hostal which has a good terrace that is

Eivissa's cathedral was originally founded about 700 years ago

open to non-residents for drinks and for a look at the surrounding views.

The last section of the Dalt Villa which should be covered is the summit of the hill, an area that is partially walled and which contains the cathedral, the remains of the town's castle and the Archaeological Museum, a building which used to be Ibiza's University. The University flourished for a short period in the 18th century. Plagues and piracy contributed to the decline of the island's economy at the time and the University never attained great importance. In the 19th century, when regular steamships linked Ibiza with Mallorca, the classrooms were closed down as students moved to the larger island.

The cathedral, **Catedral de Santa Maria de las Neus**, is disappointing, for it was almost totally knocked down and then uninspiringly rebuilt early in the 18th century. Only the tower and the apse remain of what had once been a good-looking Gothic church, built between the 13th and 16th centuries. As for the **castle**, all that is left of it is a small portion of the keep.

The **Archaeological Museum** houses a very good collection of Carthaginian remains. Digs in Ibiza have tended to yield extremely rich Punic remains, because the island was never properly Romanised and the Carthaginians carried on with their customs and lifestyle under a token Roman jurisdiction. The museum displays gravestones, terracotta statues, ceramics, glass objects, coins and other exhibits which, together, give a fairly complete vision of Punic civilisation.

For more Punic remains you should visit the **Puig des Molins Archaeological Museum**, which is in an area called Puig des Molins, lying outside the Dalt Villa between the Avenida de España, which leads to the airport and the sea. This museum is on the site of the Carthaginian Necropolis and here you can see a vast range of everyday Punic artefacts – from shaving razors to babies' bottles.

◆◆◆

LA MARINA

In this very typical Eivissa quarter, along the quayside where the ferry boats leave for Formentera and for Palma de Mallorca, Barcelona, Alicante and Valencia, you will see a cross-section of humanity acting out its different parts on Ibiza's extraordinary stage. Along the waterfront there are cafés and terraces and people milling around; in the narrow streets, set back from the harbour, there are trendy shops and even more people pacing unhurriedly about. Situated at the foot of the Dalt Villa's hill and outside its walls, this used to be the fishermen's and sailors' quarter. The seamen have long since made way for the international flotsam and jetsam which has moved in to La Marina and crowded it with art galleries, bars and boutiques.

More than picture viewing,

shopping and drinking, what most people really do in this quarter is to stare: all over the La Marina district there are people either staring or being stared at, because this is the place where the 'people watchers' and the exhibitionists of one form or

La Marina, with its trendy shops, shoppers and people-watchers, is the place to be seen in Eivissa

another meet head-on. The action takes place on the Calle Garrijo, which is the street giving onto the quayside on the right of the Formentera boat jetty, and it carries on into the streets behind and running parallel to it, the Carrer d'enrring and the Calle de la Virgen.

La Marina degenerates into a district called **Sa Penya** as you move west towards the harbour opening and the edge of the town. It may look picturesque from a distance but this area is really insalubrious and even sordid. Peopled in part by those who really have 'dropped out' with a vengeance in Ibiza, Sa Penya is not a particularly safe area, either. If, however, you like the wild side of life, these are the winding streets which permit you to sample it.

Between the jetty and the Paseo Vara de Rey, outrageous Ibiza comes in better packaging; there is no semblance of hostility and nobody feels threatened.

Beaches

If you are staying in Eivissa you have, close at hand, the Talamanca beach on the northern exit to the town on the other side of the port; and the Playa de Figueretes, heading south. Beyond Figueretes lie Playa d'en Bossa, which is noted for its celebrity bar, KU Beach; Playa d'es Cavallet, famed for being the first of Ibiza's beaches which tolerated nudists; and finally, the salt flats which form the Playa de las Salinas, and which have a very high concentration of nudists.

All these beaches are within easy striking distance by car and have good parking

facilities, and are also served by city buses. The beaches likewise have open cafés-cum-bars which are called *chiringuitos*, serving fast food, snacks and that great Balearic Islands standby, the tomato and ham sandwich – just ask for a *bocata de tomate y jamón*.

D'EN BOSSA BEACH

Not everyone's favourite; there are better sea and beach conditions in a lot of other places. D'en Bossa's main crowd-puller is its KU Beach bar which is held to be very sophisticated – a reputation that is underpinned by its prices. It is, at any rate, a very long beach, 1½ miles (2.5km) in all, and has all the usual facilities.

D'ES CAVALLET BEACH

More than half a mile (1km) long; there are normally fewer people here, though it is easily reached by car and by bus. It is well served by *chiringuitos*, and it is a pioneer beach in Ibiza's nudism stakes.

FIGUERETES BEACH

A bit of a city beach, 780ft (240m) long Figueretes has the advantages of proximity, good parking and of services such as showers and rentals, but has the hassles of crowding and dirtiness.

LAS SALINAS

You pass the salt flats on the way here (hence the beach's name) and you will find easy

parking when you arrive.
There are all the normal
facilities – sunbed rentals,
windsurf hire and ski schools –
and there are *chiringuitos* for
all; one bar, the Malibu, is
particularly popular as topless
waitresses serve the *tapas* and
drinks. The rockier end of the
beach is nudist territory.

◆
TALAMANCA BEACH
There is not too much space
here – the beach is 330ft
(100m) long and close to the
city – and it is not over clean. It
is nonetheless handy for town
dwellers, the sand is fine and
there are windsurf and pedal
boat rentals.

Accommodation
The top hotel in terms of high
prices and supreme comforts
is **Los Molinos** (tel: 302250),
which is on Ses Figueretes
beach. **Torre del Mar** (tel:
303050), on d'en Bossa beach,
comes a close second, while
Argos (tel: 312162) and **Ibiza
Playa** (tel: 302804), on
Talamanca beach and Ses
Figueretes respectively, are
slightly more down-market. In
a different category are **La
Colina de Ibiza** (tel: 332767),
which is small, exclusive and
out of town on the road to
Santa Eulalia; and **El Corsario**,
Calle Poniente 5 (tel: 301248)
which is right in the middle of
the Dalt Villa. Neither, plainly,
are bucket-and-spade type
hotels.

Nightlife
KU 4 miles (6km) out of town
in San Rafael, is quite a bit
more than a mere

discotheque. It has a luxury
restaurant, lots of bars, a
swimming pool with a glass
bottom, squash courts and
workout gyms, boutiques, art
galleries and private rooms for
exclusive parties – and also a
disco (which is underneath the
pool). Celebrities love it.
Pachá, Paseo Maritimo,
attracts all types and ages.
Amnesia, on km 5 of the San
Antonio road, is for real ravers
in the early hours. **Anfora** and
Crisco, both in the Sa Penya
district, are gay discos; and

A civilised way to soak up the sun: café society in Eivissa

fish and seafood stews served with rice, rabbit and pork based stews, stewed courgettes, aubergines and tomatoes. It is the sort of place that locals patronise, and the prices are reasonable. **Sausalito**, on the quayside, Plaza Sarabia 5, is the opposite. It is pricey and is patronised by trendies. You might see celebrities there and if you don't see the stars you will at least get lots of candlelight. The most ambitious restaurant, as far as cooking is concerned, and also the most expensive is **Amar Lur**, which serves complex Basque-inspired nouvelle cuisine. It is just out of town on km 2.3 of the San Miguel road at Santa Gertrudis. Also out of town are **Ca'n Pau** on the San Miguel road; **Ca Na Joana**, San José, km 2.5; and **La Masia d'En Sord**, San Miguel road, km 1. These are farmhouses converted into roadside inns and they take a good deal of trouble in creating a friendly, pleasant atmosphere and in serving fairly imaginative Catalan and Balearic food.

Bars and cafés are plentiful: **La Maravilla**, on the Plaza de la Constitución, opens at 06.00 and serves tomato sandwiches and other life restorers for swinging people who have been up all night. **Mar y Sol** by the port on Paseo del Puerto, brings together crowds of beautiful people and the people watchers. **Bar Estrella**, on Plaza Antonio Riquer, by the ferry jetty, is the place for the first or the last drink on the

the **Casino de Ibiza**, on the Paseo Maritimo, has a nightclub, restaurant, and snack bar as well as roulette, *chemin de fer* and black jack tables.

Restaurants
Alfredo in the town centre, Paseo Vara del Rey 16, is a long established restaurant which has the dual virtue of being unpretentious and of serving honest Ibiza food – rich

island if you are arriving or leaving by boat.

Montesol, Paseo Vara del Rey 2, is a classical café and a rendezvous for the more sober residents. **Mono Desnudo** on the quayside, Calle Garijo 16, was a pioneer bar in the people-watching game and **Zoo** and **Tango**, both on Calle Pou, just off Garijo, are in the same league. **Torre del Canigó**, in the Dalt Villa, is more specifically gay than most bars in the town.

Shopping

In Ibiza there is a lot more to buy than the usual holiday resort souvenirs. Some of the handicrafts on the island are exceptionally good. In addition, there is a very important local fashion industry, an Ibiza look which has come to be known as the Ad Lib fashion.

Handicrafts

Ibiza, like everywhere else in Spain, has a long artisan and craft tradition. The difference between Ibiza and the rest of the country is that whereas artisans have been on the wane elsewhere, in Ibiza they have been injected with new lifeblood by the arrival of the cosmopolitan crowd of craftsmen who have set up shop on the island.

The traditional handicrafts on the island, even since Punic times, have been weaving, spinning and working with clay. What you are going to find in Ibiza are basket and *esparto* grass products, from hats to *espadrilles*; rope-soled sandals also known as *alpargatas*; hand-spun woollen blankets and cotton blankets

Pottery is an age-old Ibiza craft – and it is possible to find smaller examples as souvenirs

called *jarapas*, which make good bedspreads; and ceramics of every kind.

Ibiza boasts, moreover, a long tradition of fashioning metal decorative trinkets, and nowadays this has been developed into a fairly big costume jewellery, and also leather goods, handicraft industry. What strikes most people about the Ibiza products is the originality of the designs – the 'hippy' culture which descended on Ibiza in the 1960s, seemed to form a successful marriage with artefacts handed down by the Carthaginians, the Romans and the Moors.

To get a general impression of what is available. the best idea is to wander around the quayside open-air market, called the *mercadillo*, that packs in the crowds by Eivissa's port every afternoon and evening, Monday to Saturday.

For specific shopping, recommended establishments include **S'Espardanya**, Calle Ignacio de Riquer 19, in the Dalt Villa, for rope-soled sandals; and **Es Piló** in the same street for rugs and blankets.

Also in the Dalt Villa, just as you enter it by the Portal de las Tablas gateway, you will find **El Mohán** on the Plaza de la Villa. This very popular store sells just about everything from clothes to paintings by way of ceramics. There are millions of *espadrilles* for sale, some of them ultra modern, at **Casa Catalina**, Calle Montgri 2, in the La Marina district (the street starts at the port); and straw hats, baskets and the rest are sold at **Casa José Viñas**, which is on Calle de la Cruz 34, a street leading off Montgri and running parallel to the quayside, and which is also known as the Sa Creu street.

If you are seriously interested in good ceramics you should look in on the prestigious workshops, **Taller Daifa** and **Taller Frigoles**, which are both in the district called Barrio de Can Bufi on the road to San Antonio.

Fashion

What you should be looking for is the so-called Ad Lib line of clothes. Essentially these are comfortable, very casual, eye-catching and original clothes which base their designs and shapes and even their material on what were originally the local islanders' garments. Ad Lib, once upon a time, drew closely from its genuine roots, but the fashion line has increasingly come to cover a multitude of sins, to the point that anything which is slightly unusual but plausibly wearable is now dubbed with the trade mark.

There are plenty of clothes stores, especially in the La Marina area. You should proceed slowly from the Paseo Vara de Rey along the Calle Rimbau and Sa Creu (or de la Cruz), along Calle Mayor and Calle de la Virgen and, once you have strolled along such streets, double back to enter the shops that appealed to you. The stores where people buy clothes in order to show off and to be looked at are mostly to be found in the La Marina quarter. One thing to remember is that what is normal, even boring and essential, dress in Ibiza could be totally out of place, outrageous and absurd, if worn anywhere else. Ibiza can demand its own special uniform, which is readily available. Top establishments include **Pink Fly** on Calle Rimbau 4, **Por Qué No**, on Rimbau 25, **Maria M**, which has shops on Riambau 2 and Calle de la Virgen 29; **Paula's** on Calle de la Virgen 4, **Aubergine and Co**, which is at number 36, **Ibiza Lights**, number 40, and **Gerry Kelly**, which is right at the end of the same street. On the Calle Mayor, shops include **Y Atzi**, number 10, **Dora Herbst** at number 12 and **Eva Drake** at number 23. On Sa Creu shops include **Tip Top** at number 16, **The End**, number 26 and **NYC Saldos**, which is next door at number 28.

THE NORTHERN COAST OF IBIZA

For holidaymakers this part of the island is dominated by two resorts: **San Antonio Abad**, on the west of the island and linked to Eivissa by the C-731; and **Portinatx**, in the north and joined to the capital by the C-733. These stand for mass tourism, and for some of the worst land speculation and construction abuse on the island.

When it is packed out in high summer with young northern Europeans, San Antonio becomes more of a sociological phenomenon than a tourist resort.

Unless you want to join these crowds, the only reason to go to San Antonio Abad is in order to hire a boat or join a boat excursion that will take you well away from the place along the northern coast of the island to Portinatx. San Antonio, or San Ant as the tourists prefer to call it, is unquestionably a superb natural harbour, and its bay is chock-a-block with boats.

The easiest way of enjoying the indisputable delights of the San Antonio-Portinatx stretch of coastline is the seaward route, but you can also, with varying amounts of difficulty, approach at least some of the northern coast's coves and inlets by land. The latter means a certain amount of trekking from base camps in the villages of San Mateo and San Miguel.

The best idea is probably to check out the lie of the coast and its *calas* (inlets) first by way of a San Antonio-Portinatx ferry boat ride and then to tackle your selected cove from the land.

FERRY CRUISES

There are a number of ferries leaving San Antonio's quay daily around 10.00 hrs for Portinatx. Some boats stop and drop people off at various coves, and pick them up on the return trip in the afternoon. The sea trip takes you along the mostly virgin coast of northern Ibiza. The

The coves of Portinatx have been 'discovered' – but not spoilt

disadvantage is, naturally, that you are at the mercy of the ferry boat service.

An alternative involves forming a small party of like-minded souls and paying about 30,000 pesetas between you to rent your own yacht for the day, along with its captain. You may be able to hire a fishing boat and this involves chatting up likely candidates on San Antonio's quayside.

There are several excursion possibilities, depending on whether you aim to go on a cruise along the coast or whether you just want to spend the day in a specific *cala*, or inlet, that is virtually inaccessible except by sea. The overriding consideration is that Ibiza is a whole new experience if you are circling it by sea – and this is also true of every other Balearic island. Leaving the bay of San Antonio bound for Portinatx, the first major landmark is the **Cala Gració** which is very developed and therefore exceedingly popular and crowded. 'San Ant' spills over into it. Cala Gració is a reference point of the Ibiza of today, compared with the Ibiza that once was, and you will

A typically attractive village scene on Ibiza: San Mateo

understand this contrast as you proceed further along the route.

After passing the **Cabo Negret** promontory, the shoreline becomes first implausibly terraced and then, more believably, wild. Landmarks include two tiny isles called **Ses Margalides** and the high, 1,200ft (375m) cliff called the **Joan Andreu Cliff**, which is one of the highest points on the island. The cruise takes you past one inlet after another. The most amazing of all the *calas* is a particularly deep and wide one, certainly virtually inaccessible by land, called **Cala Aubarca**. This is the sort of place that guarantees the solitude that Ibiza *aficionados* go on about so much. It is a hallowed spot.

Mediterranean beauty continues now for a while and the cruise passes by the super luxury hotel Hacienda Na

Xamena, which is an example of how a development, far from wrecking the environment, may actually enhance it (see **Accommodation**, below). Hopes of continuing sensitivity from the developers are, however, soon wrecked by a series of resorts linked to the town of San Miguel and before long you arrive at **Portinatx**. The astonishing thing about the latter's couple of coves is that they have not been spoilt in their essentials – a good beach and clean water – by the surrounding land speculation.

LAND ROUTES

You can reach Cala Aubarca by land if you make your way first to the village of **San Mateo**, near the larger village of **Santa Inés**, and then take a forestry road that leads towards the coast and which starts close by San Mateo's parish church. **Cala Aubarca** is some 2½ miles (4km) away and this includes a half-mile (1km) cliff-top scramble to the cove. You are well advised not to drive your car up to the cliffs, for the surface there is unsafe; it is better to leave your vehicle in the forest. Be sure to wear suitable footwear and give yourself time for the trek back up the cliffs.

The cove of **Es Penyals de s'Aguila** is another example of the more or less solitary places you can get to if you are willing to make the effort. Take the road from San Miguel to San Mateo and stay on it, past the left turn off to San Mateo, until you reach the Isla Blanca urbanisation. It is best to leave your car around here and to follow the path to Es Penyals. **Es Canaret** is, by contrast, a relatively simple expedition. This cove is close to the San Marça caves, which you reach along a well signposted road from San Miguel. Leave your car at the caves' parking lot, and the cove is spread out below you. The caves are open to the public and the visit to them includes a *son et lumière*.

Accommodation

Perhaps the most remarkable hotel in this area is the **Hacienda Na Xamena** (tel: 334500). Part of the Na Xamena development and set on a promontory of the same name, this hotel is far and away the most luxurious, scenically situated and exclusive on the island. Its terraced bars and restaurants are open to non-residents.

Nightlife

The flow of San Antonio's evening crowds will sooner or later propel you into a disco such as **Estudio 7**, on Avenida Dr Fleming or **Es Paradis Terrenal** at Pasaje Can Maña in the Ses Jonqueres district. The latter club has a confusing number of pulsating, strobe-flashing dance floors filling up its large grounds, and those who patronise them would agree that the club is, as its name proclaims, 'Paradise on Earth'.

Restaurants

If you want to experience the San Antonio youth

phenomenon at first hand just head for the Avenida Dr Fleming and join the ebb and flow of the human tide on a warm evening as it samples *cuba libre* (rum and Coke or Bacardi and Coke) drinking and hot dog munching in one terrace café and fast food joint after another.

A couple of rather more exclusive restaurants are, however, worth noting. **Rias Baixas** Ignacio Riquer 4, is run by Galicians and serves the fish-based food of that northwest, Celtic region of Peninsular Spain. Seafood which is flown in specially from Galicia, and claims in particular, figure highly on the menu.

Sa Capella (open only for dinners) serves mostly French-inspired food in a pleasant little old building that is stuffed with local antiques. The building was apparently intended to serve as a church, but was never properly completed, and it stands outside the town at km 0.5 on the road to Can Coix.

INLAND IBIZA

Apart from wanting to get away from crowds, you can adopt a positive approach to touring inland Ibiza. Parts of the island are extremely unspoilt; with their olive and almond groves, the fig and the carob trees and the scented air of wild herbs, they are an authentic showcase for a very specific type of Mediterranean landscape.

One striking feature is the very red colour of the earth. Enthusiasts of such russet-tinged clods of land, such as the poet Federigo García Lorca, claimed that they would like to spread them over their bread as if they were patés or, more exact, the local spicy *sobrasada* spread.

The best view of the island is to be had from the summit of the Atalayasa hill, which can be reached by taking a winding dirt road that starts on your left just outside San José, in the south of the island. From here you can see the Valencian coast of the Spanish mainland.

Arguably the best rural drive on the island is the route along the northwest between San Miguel and Santa Inés. The best picture-postcard features of the *Ibicenco* landscape lie along this 12-mile (20km) trip.

WHAT TO SEE

BALAFI

Set between San Juan and San Lorenzo, this village is one of Ibiza's prides. With its tiny alleyways and glistening cottages, it is a very old and extremely evocative little hamlet. Balafi's houses are clustered round two defensive towers, which is where the locals gathered when their rural arcadia was threatened by Turkish pirate raids. The origins of the village are said to date back to Carthaginian times. You will certainly have to park your car outside the village and walk into it.

Well away from the pace-setting crowds of Ibiza's towns, there is still some stunning scenery

◆◆◆
JESÚS

The church in the village of Jesús makes the justifiable claim of possessing the most important art treasure on the entire island, the church's altarpiece, called the **Virgen de los Angeles**. The work is an intriguing mix of gothic and Renaissance styles and it is thought to have been executed at the beginning of the 16th century. Your eyes are drawn first to the altarpiece's base, which traces, in each of its seven sections, key events in the life of the Virgin Mary: from the Annunciation to the

Assumption by way of the Nativity, the Epiphany, the Resurrection, the Ascension and Pentecost. Moving up the middle of the altarpiece there is a representation of the Virgin and Child; above that, one of the stigmatisation of St Francis; and, finally, at the top, a popular scene from the life of Saint Gregory in which Christ, crowned with a halo, appears as Gregory is saying Mass. The side panels of this complex structure shows more scenes from the lives of diverse saints. The church, with all its treasures, is often locked, but there should be no difficulty about asking a local for the key. Alternatively, turn up when there is a service going on and explain to the priest that you would be interested in seeing the altarpiece – *retablo* in Spanish. To reach Jesús turn right off a side road 1½ miles (2.5km) out of Ibiza on the road to Santa Eulalia.

◆◆
SANTA GERTRUDIS

Santa Gertrudis is somewhat spoilt by the inevitable housing developments; these have encroached inland just as much as they have gobbled up so many parts of the coast. It is worth visiting, nonetheless, for its shopping. On the main square, the **Plaza de la Iglesia**, stands the church; and on the streets leading out of it there are

a number of boutiques and antique shops which sell everything from second hand books to old mirrors and costume jewellery (see **Shopping**, below). Take a left turn to the village on to the San Miguel road, 4 miles (6km) out of Ibiza on the C-733 to Santa Eulalia and Portinatx.

◆◆
SAN MIGUEL

This village boasts one of the oldest churches on the island, for its foundations date from the 14th century. The building is a

The limewashed church of San Miguel was once a refuge for villagers during pirate raids

good example of the fortified churches that sprung up all over Ibiza; church buildings in Ibiza served as much to protect parishioners physically during pirate raids as they did to administer to their spiritual needs. The porch and the patio of the San Miguel church date from the 18th century.

Restaurants
For an inland restaurant with a view, visit the **Grill San Rafael**, in the village of San Rafael, which is 4 miles (7km) out of Ibiza on the C-731 to San Antonio. Set in a garden just by the church, this is held by many to be the best restaurant on the island. The main view is of the town of Ibiza and on a clear day you can see the island of Formentera.

Shopping
Santa Gertrudis is the best bet for interesting shops. **El Almacén** and **La Luna**, both on the Plaza de la Iglesia, are interesting for home decoration artefacts and **Punto A** on the main street that runs through the village specialises in accessory knick knacks.

THE EAST COAST OF IBIZA

In the summer the population of the east coast of Ibiza swells enormously as tourists head for its popular resorts, but it is possible, even in the holiday centres, to find quieter attractions.

ES CANA
Just 2½ miles (4km) north of the

large town of Santa Eulalia (see below), Es Cana is a very popular resort built around a big beach and among pine woods. One of the attractions of the town that brings in visitors from all over the island is the open air crafts market which is staged every Wednesday. There is an amazing array of ceramics, leather goods, costume jewellery, trinkets of every kind and off-the-peg clothes on offer.

The **d'es Cana beach** is especially crowded in the high season because it is close to a popular local camp site (there are two of them in the Santa Eulalia and Es Cana area). Alternative beaches are **Cala Nova** and, a bit further north, **Cala Llena**, which can be reached by a coastal path.

SAN CARLOS
A trip to this extremely agreeable little town brings you immediately into rural Ibiza and the countryside here is perfect. In San Carlos the **church** is worth a second look. Built in the 18th century, it is less stumpy than is the norm on the island, and has a particularly beautiful porch.

You should also look out for **Anita's Bar**, Junto a la Iglesia, once famed as a meeting place for the hippies and flower children who flocked to Ibiza in the brave old days.

Just by Anita's Bar the road forks, leading to the beach of Cala Mastella, the right fork, and to Cala Boix. **Cala Mastella** used to be one of the shared secret coves for those who really knew their Ibiza. It is no longer quite that, for word has got around that in addition to being an enchanting inlet, it is also the bolt hole for Mr Joan Ferrer, alias Bigotis or Moustaches. Ferrer is a fisherman and also a cook; he transforms his daily catch into superlative fish stews called *bullit de peix* and serves his concoctions up in his open air bar, the **Tio Bigotis Chiringuito**, El Rigoto, Can Jordi, which stands in a corner of the Cala Mastella inlet. Cala Mastella is somewhat protected, because the road stops a good half mile (1km) short of the cove and you have to walk the last part. The water is very clean here and it is darkened by the landscape that presses in and hangs over the inlet. The beach itself is pretty small, some 55 yards (50m) long and less than 11 yards (10m) wide. Apart from the *chiringuito*, there is not a building in sight.

Access is easier to **Cala Boix**, which is well signposted and has a parking lot. A staircase leads down to the cove, where there are two restaurants, a *chiringuito* and sunbeds and other facilities. The sand is dark and the water is magnificently clear. On your approach to Cala Boix (a fine drive through red earth fields and olive and almond tree groves) you will pass a turning off to Pou del Lleó and to the **Playa de Aigües Blanques**.

The latter is another fine beach with a restaurant and good rental facilities, including windsurf hire. The parking lot is somewhat back from the shore and reaching the beach does involve a bit of a climb. The beach is very popular with nude sunbathers and there are some rocky islets off it which are popular with swimmers.

◆◆
SANTA EULALIA DEL RÍO

This is the largest town on the island after Eivissa, and is on the estuary of the island's only river, hence the *del Río* handle to its name. The river is, in fact, just a dry bed, but elderly locals swear that gurgling water once flowed along it.

To restore a sense of balance in Santa Eulalia, which, in the high season, rivals San Antonio for young crowds of tourists, you could do a lot worse than to visit the **Puig**, or mountain, **de Missa**. This is a very unspoilt part of the island, doubly remarkable for being close to an area that has been largely wrecked. On top of the hill and commanding a panoramic view there is a group of houses, clustered round a 16th-century church like chickens around a hen. Puig de Missa's church and its satellite cottages have a fortified air to them, and this illustrates the times when the islanders retreated back from the coast at the slightest hint of pirates on the horizon. Cannons used to be fired from the walls by the church. You might visit the village's **cemetery**, and for a bit of cultural uplift there is the **Barrau Museum**, with works by local impressionist painters. The top of the Puig can be reached by turning right, just beyond the petrol station on the coast road to Eivissa.

In the style of all good resorts Santa Eulalia is within striking distance of good bucket-and-spade beach sites, and it does boast its own town beach which is flanked by fast food joints. Just north of Santa Eulalia you can opt between the **Playa de Niu Blau** and the fairly narrow strand of **Cala Pada**. Both beaches have restaurants, bars and full facilities. South of the town, towards Eivissa, you can choose between **Playa de Caló de S'Alga** and **Cala Llonga**, a cove which has pine trees, but also buildings, extending almost right down to the sea shore. Both these beaches, again, are properly equipped with bar and sea sport rentals.

Street cafés in Santa Eulalia

Accommodation

The quieter establishments in Santa Eulalia are the **Fenicia**, (tel: 330101) one of the resort's two four-star hotels, which is out of town at the Siesta urbanisation in Ca'n Fita. The best of the three-star range in terms of avoiding the fairground-cum-holiday camp atmosphere are arguably **Sol S'Argamassa** at the S'Argamassa urbanisation (tel: 330075) and **Tres Torres**, in the Ses Estaques quarter (tel: 330326). All three hotels, as is the norm in Ibiza's resorts, are closed from November to March.

Restaurants

There are a couple of good places to eat in Santa Eulalia: **Donya Margarita** is one of the landmarks on the Paseo Maritimo, and **El Naranjo** is on

Calle Sant Josep 31. The former sticks closer to traditional island fare, such as rice dishes, while the latter boasts a more adventurous kitchen. The two are heading towards being pricey but do take all the major credit cards.

A good selection of bars is available in the resort. **Mozart** is a popular and fun bar just next door to El Naranjo on the Calle Sant Josep; **Top Hat** on Avenida Isidro Macabich 4, draws both residents and visitors; and **Pussy Cat**, Paseo de la Alameda, is partly a bar and partly a boutique.

THE SOUTH COAST OF IBIZA

The base camp for Ibiza's south coast is the inland little town of San José, which stands close to the 1,558ft (475m) high Atalayasa mountain (the island's biggest) and lies 12 miles (19km) from Eivissa. From here it is possible to visit a number of natural attractions.

WHAT TO SEE

CALA D'HORT

Just beyond San José, on the road to San Antonio, a left turn towards the coast takes you to Cala d'Hort cove. The last part of the 4 mile (6km) road is unsurfaced and should be treated with caution. Cala d'Hort is one of Ibiza's showpiece coves, because it has two impressive rock islands: **Isla Vedrá** the bigger one, and **Isla Vendranell**, which both look pretty close to the beach until you start trying

to swim towards them; take your time. Myths surrounding the twin isles include one that has them as the home of sirens who bewitched Ulysses; and another that claims they are the location of a secret energy-giving pyramid that is used by Martians. What is proven is that the rocks are a nesting ground for a great number of sea birds.

COVA SANTA

Close by San José's Ca Na Joana restaurant, and $5\frac{1}{2}$ miles (9km) out of Eivissa, a left turn onto a paved road leads to one of the island's most interesting caves. Called the **Cova Santa**, or Holy Cave, because a hermit once lived there, the cavern was used as a hideout by local peasants during pirate raids. It is all of 82ft (25m) deep and its waters are said to have healing powers. Near the cave, a passable track leads to the pebbly beach of **Cala Yondal**, where there are rarely many people, although facilities include sunbed rentals, a *chiringuito* beach bar and pedal boats.

Accommodation

San José has a number of three-star hotels, including **Milford I Fiesta** (tel: 340612) and **Milford II Fiesta** (tel: 341227), which both have tennis facilities.

Restaurants

There are several bars in the town of San José, and the best restaurant, **Ca Na Joana**, is situated on km 10 of the Eivissa-San José road.

FORMENTERA

Just 32 square miles (82sq km) and stretching only 12 miles (19km) at its widest point, Formentera is the smallest of the Balearic Islands and is more of a day-trip isle than a holiday resort. It is certainly the most unspoilt inhabited area of the Balearics. The vegetation – fig and almond trees, corn and vineyards – is very similar to that of Ibiza, and the real difference is that there are fewer people and considerably fewer fast food joints and touristy excesses. The island's name is a corruption of *Frumentum*, from the Latin for wheat, for the Romans knew it as the 'wheat isle'. Abandoned during the Middle Ages, Formentera was repopulated in the late-17th century and is now extremely well linked to Ibiza by a succession of ferry boats. Its economy is based on agriculture, a certain amount of tourism and on arts and crafts.

Approaches to Formentera

Boats leave for Formentera from most of Ibiza's ports, but Eivissa offers the most regular

The work goes on for some: fishing nets are prepared in La Sabina

service (as many as 20 trips a day), as well as the quickest route. The ferries leave Ibiza from the Paseo Maritimo, the main quayside of the port, and they dock in Formentera at La Sabina about an hour later (a hydrofoil takes only 25 minutes). If you take the ferry, make sure that it goes to La Sabina (some go to specific beaches), because La Sabina is the only place on Formentera where you will be able to hire transport. At La Sabina there are car, motorscooter and bicycle rentals.

WHAT TO SEE

◆◆
CAN NA COSTA
Near San Fernando, which is in the centre of the island at its narrowest point, this megalithic sepulchre is one of the most important monuments in the whole of the Balearics, for it is a key indicator of Bronze Age settlements on this group of islands.

◆◆◆
LA MOLA
For a bird's eye view of the island you should drive or ride from La Sabina to the La Mola lighthouse, which is on the easternmost tip of Formentera. From this area, a mini plateau called La Mola which is 630ft (192m) high, you can see the whole island and decide exactly where you want to go next. The route to the lighthouse is on the island's only main road, which passes through **San Francisco**, the

The stuff of city-dwellers' dreams: getting away from it all

village which serves as Formentera's capital, and also wends its way through San Fernando, situated in the middle of the island.

herons are common, and towards the end of the summer flamingos make a usually brief appearance, providing an exotic treat.

Beaches

The longest beach on the island is **Mitjorn**, which follows a wide bay on the south of the island. This is a pebbly beach. The beach of **Es Pujols**, by the promontory called Punta Prima and close to La Sabina, is sandy, and **Cala Sahona**, in the west of the island, is the most touristy. Near La Sabina and just by Illetas there are several beaches on either side of the spindly finger of land, pointing towards Ibiza, that leads to the Punta des Trocadors promontory. The water on the western side of the finger tends to be somewhat rougher.

Accommodation

The island's only four-star hotel is the **Iberotel Club la Mola**, on Mitjorn beach (tel: 328069). On the same beach is the three-star **Formentera Playa** (tel: 320000). The two-star **Cala Saona** (tel: 322030) is on the cove of the same name.

Shopping

A very popular Sunday arts and crafts market is held close by the hamlet of **El Pilar** in La Mola. The quality of the jewellery, leather goods, blankets, hand knitted sweaters and ceramics sold there is held to be good, although the prices are not especially competitive. The arts and crafts community lives mostly in El Pilar, and you can inspect workshops during weekdays.

◆◆◆
LAS SALINAS

The Las Salinas salt flats, near La Sabina, are particularly interesting because, like their counterpart on Ibiza, they attract a variety of bird life. Egrets, mallard ducks and

PEACE AND QUIET

Countryside and Wildlife on the Balearic Islands
By Paul Sterry

The Balearic Islands offer unique opportunities to anyone interested in wildlife. They hold most of the key plants, animals and habitats of the region and, being so popular with visitors from northern Europe, are within easy reach.

The reason for the amazing wealth of wildlife found on the islands is the variety of habitats. These range from sand dunes and cliffs around the coast to open areas of scrub and woodland to mountains of nearly 5,000ft (1,500m) and all can be seen in a day's drive. Mallorca alone boasts a flowering plant list of nearly 1,300 species, 40 of which are found nowhere else in the world.

The climate of the islands is typically Mediterranean, with hot, dry summers and mild winters. Despite the proximity of the sea, which helps moderate the extremes in temperature, the winters can feel decidedly chilly and snow is not unknown.

The garigue habitat which comprises the interior of most of the Balearics is rich in wildlife

The Character of the Islands

Mallorca is by far the largest of the main Balearic Islands, covering an area of over 1,400 square miles (3,600sq km). The other main islands in decreasing order of size are Menorca, Ibiza, Formentera and Cabrera, and there are numerous small islets in the region. The order roughly corresponds to the islands' natural history interest in terms of variety of habitat and species, with Mallorca again coming out top. Despite its vast holiday developments, central and northern Mallorca has remained largely unscathed. Although less varied, the other islands all have plenty to offer the wildlife enthusiast.

The Mediterranean climate, and in particular the sun, is a major influence on the wildlife. Most animals avoid the heat of the midday sun and tend to forage in the mornings and evenings. The summer sun can be excessively hot, and some animals even go into a state of summer hibernation called 'aestivation', from which they wake in the autumn. Most conspicuous of these are the snails which festoon branches and twigs in the height of summer.

The major problem that the Mediterranean sun poses to plants is that of water loss, and you will soon notice that many of them have thick, waxy leaves to prevent evaporation. The other problem they face is grazing by animals, and in particular by that scourge of the Mediterranean, the introduced feral goat.

To discourage animals from eating them, many plants have developed strongly aromatic flavours. Although this works with most species, it has had the opposite of the desired effect on humans, with plants such as rosemary and thyme being sought as culinary aids. In the open, stony areas known as *garigue*, many of the little cushion plants possess fearsome spines with the same aim of discouraging grazing animals.

The animal that has had the most significant effect upon the appearance of the Balearic Islands is, of course, man. Over the course of centuries he has cleared much of the evergreen forest which would once have cloaked the islands. His animals, and particularly his goats, have prevented all but the hardiest plants from regaining more than a foothold. Today, the main threat to the environment of the islands still comes from man, but now in the form of direct tourist development coupled with the vastly increased water demand for the visitors.

The Coasts
Conspicuous by their absence are the vast numbers of seabirds that might be expected with the wealth of marine life in the surrounding seas. The reason for this lies in the nature of the Mediterranean sea itself. Since there is little tidal range in this land-locked sea and the small inter-tidal range that does get exposed is baked by the sun, the hostile environment defeats most forms of marine life and there is little for birds to feed on. However, there are still birds to be seen, the most common being the herring gull. This is not the more familiar bird of northern Europe, however, because here they have bright yellow, not pink, legs. Occasionally they are joined by one of the world's rarest birds, the Audouin's gull. It is smaller than its relative, with a red beak and dark legs, and the Balearics are one of its remaining strongholds.

During periods of onshore winds, any exposed rocky coast can be good for watching seabirds. The Balearic race of the Manx shearwater is common and it is sometimes joined by the larger Cory's shearwater. Both are masters of the sea breezes, but are vulnerable on land. Consequently, they breed in cliff burrows and only come ashore to visit them at night.

PEACE AND QUIET

Coastal cliffs are also good for pallid swifts, paler and browner than the common swifts which also occur. But most impressive of all are the Eleonora's falcons, long-winged predators that haunt the impressive cliffs of Cabo Formentor in Mallorca as well as many other sites. Many of the beaches have a good selection of drift shells, including the well-known murex. In Roman times, the body of the animal was used to obtain royal purple, with which togas were dyed. You may also notice curious ball-shaped objects on the tideline. These are the matted remains of a sea-grass called *posidonia*, common around Mediterranean shores. In addition to Cape Formentor, another good coastal site to visit is Porto Colom on the southwest coast of Mallorca. Visit both the harbour – for unusual gulls – and the peninsula – for Marmora's warblers and seabirds. On Menorca, visit the Playa de Binimel'la area for stunning cliff scenery. The southwest coast of Ibiza is still unspoilt. The coastal scrub has flowers, birds and Ibiza wall lizards. Seabirds can be seen out to sea.

Cory's shearwaters are clumsy on land but masters of flight. Small groups of birds are often seen passing headlands and cliffs

Freshwater Marshes

Many marshes have been drained, but the Albufera and Albufereta on Mallorca are still wonderful places to visit. In addition, the many small wetland habitats which you may come across in your travels will all hold something of interest.
The first thing that you will notice when you enter one of the larger marshes is the noise. A chorus of marsh frogs and green toads competes with an amazing selection of warblers, including moustached, Cetti's, Savi's, reed and great reed. The latter has a particularly deep and a frog-like voice and it is often difficult to tell whether the caller is a bird or an amphibian.
One bird that is typical of the Balearics is the diminutive fan-tailed warbler. Although seldom seen as more than a dot in the sky, it is one of the easiest birds to identify.
Throughout most of the spring

and summer, the males sing their characteristic 'zip-zip-zip' song which is uttered while they fly vertically up and down. They look, to all intents and purposes, like yo-yos!

In open areas of marsh, migrant sandpipers feed alongside long-legged black-winged stilts and little egrets.

The Albufereta marshes lie beside the road from Puerto de Pollença to Alcudia. To reach the more extensive Albufera, take the road from Alcudia towards Artá. Park on the coastal side of the road under the pines, cross the road and walk along the wide track on the banks of a large drainage channel.

The abundance of fish and amphibians attracts a variety of predators other than the birds.

Most frequently seen is the viperine snake, a large and boldly marked species, which likes to sunbathe on dry ground. In the water channels, European pond terrapins also take their toll of small fish and frogs.

A description of the marshes would not be complete without mention of the insect life. Myriad small flies provide food for tens of thousands of migrant swallows and other hirundines that stop off. These insects also provide food for the abundant dragonflies which, in turn, are caught by visiting Eleonora's falcons. Most colourful of all the marshes' insects must surely be the swallowtail butterfly, with its yellow, black and red wings. Its yellow and black caterpillars are often found on their favourite foodplant, fennel.

PEACE AND QUIET

Open Country

A significant proportion of the woodland which once covered the Balearics has been cleared over the centuries, leaving a variety of open habitats. Areas which have not been cultivated vary in appearance from the bushy scrub, called *maquis*, to the barren, stony habitat known as *garigue*.

Maquis is characterised by bushy plants such as rosemary, broom, rock-roses and lavenders, and is noted for its aroma, so characteristic of the

The swallowtail is a large and colourful butterfly which can be found in flowery meadows from April until June

Mediterranean region. Occasional olive trees provide shade for the ubiquitous Sardinian warbler, a year-round resident and one of the commonest birds of the Balearics. Its harsh call and conspicuous red eye-ring make it easy to identify. In open patches of *maquis*, trefoils, restharrows, gladioli and several species of orchid add variety and colour.

Garigue habitat is, by contrast, much more barren in appearance. However, what its plants lack in lushness, they make up for in variety of shape and form. To resist water loss in an already dry environment, many form dense, compact clumps with tightly packed leaves and flowers which would be the envy of many Alpine gardeners. They are frequently referred to as 'hedgehog' plants because of their shape and the abundance of vicious spines, which also protect against grazing animals. Larger bushes may harbour Marmora's warblers, a speciality of the Balearic Islands. Listen for the scratchy song and eventually the bird may hop on top of the bush. Insect life is much in evidence in these open habitats. Grasshoppers and bush-crickets are abundant, often falling victim to the voracious appetites of the many lizards. Butterflies such as the painted lady and clouded yellow flit from flower to flower and are sometimes joined by the day flying silvery moth and the hummingbird hawk moth. The latter is an amazing sight as it

The monotonous night-time call of the Scop's owl sounds like a sonar 'blip' and readily reveals the bird's roosting site

feeds on the wing with its long proboscis probing the flowers for nectar.

Cashing in on this abundance of insect life is the most colourful bird of the Balearics, the bee-eater. These birds are summer visitors to the Mediterranean from April to September. Some stay to breed in excavated holes in sand pits but many more pass through on their way north.

Evergreen Forests

In the Mediterranean evergreen trees predominate over trees which shed their leaves in the autumn. Their thick, waxy leaves are resistant to dessication, and by retaining their leaves throughout the year they can grow during the cooler, wetter period from September to May. Unfortunately, evergreen woodland now covers only a fraction of the area that it covered before the arrival of man in the Balearics, and today's woodlands fall into two very distinct types.

Aleppo pine forests are widespread around the sandy coasts and on many hills. They are light and airy with plenty of clearings. In contrast, holm oak woodland is dense and shady. Holm oaks prefer areas with higher rainfall and are,

PEACE AND QUIET

Large, showy plants of hellebore often adorn roadside verges in the more rural areas of the islands

rather like sonar blips, which are the 'songs' of Scop's owls.

During the daytime the birds are seemingly invisible due to their amazing camouflage. Pine woodland ground flora is rich, with tongue orchids and naked man orchids being conspicuous. Large cobweb tents in trees stripped of foliage are the work of the caterpillars of the pine processionary moth. When these colonial caterpillars have stripped their host tree they descend to the ground and march in procession to the next one.

The ground flora of holm oak woodland can be rather sparse by comparison. It is dominated by ferns and mosses but the bright red berries of butcher's broom add a splash of colour, and cyclamens grow among rocks in more open spots. There are pockets of woodland all over the north and east of Mallorca. Good areas can be found midway between Puerto de Pollença and the Formentor peninsula. Park off the road and do not leave valuables in your car. The track which leads down to Torrent de Pareis, along the north coast, is also well wooded. As a general rule, strips of coastal woodland in developed parts of Mallorca are too disturbed for most wildlife.

therefore, more or less confined to the northern sierras and Artá peninsula of Mallorca.

In spring, the lowland woodlands come alive with the songs of nightingales and serins. In among all this noise, the high-pitched song of the firecrest is almost lost and you might overlook the calls of the Balearic race of the crossbill. By contrast, a visit to the same woodland at night can be rather eerie because of the strange monotonous calls,

Mountains

It is amazing to think that there are mountains on an island the size of Mallorca, but indeed, there are, and one, Puig

Mayor, rises to nearly 5,000ft (1,500m) above sea level. In fact there is a chain of mountains running along the northwest of Mallorca and the Artá peninsula has a mountain range of its own.

Mountain vegetation is rather sparse and typically like the barren, stony *garigue* found at lower elevations. Many species of 'hedgehog' plants compete for the prime sites, and spiny restharrows and hellebores seemingly grow out of bare rock. Here and there clumps of paeony and cyclamen thrive, and to complete the illusion of its being a planted rockery, the charming fairy foxglove puts in an appearance.

Mountain tops everywhere are prone to cloud cover, which obscures visibility. However, on clear days the peaks and summits of Mallorcan mountains provide superb thermals for birds of prey. All the species seen in the lowlands of the Balearics can be spotted from time to time and there is always a chance of something spectacular such as golden eagle, Bonelli's eagle or peregrine. Larger birds of prey are often mobbed by ravens, which are quite common and recognised by their harsh croaking calls and wedge-shaped tails.

Pride of place among Mallorca's birds of prey must go to the majestic black vultures. These immense birds have a wingspan of over 8ft (2.5m) and soar effortlessly for hours on end, scanning the ground for carrion. Reliable figures for their numbers in the Balearics are difficult to obtain, but recent estimates put it at over 60 birds. If you spend long enough scanning the skies in the north of Mallorca you should be lucky. In the winter they often descend to lower altitudes and have even been seen from the Boquer Valley near Puerto de Pollença.

If you walk in the hills and mountains of the Balearics it will not be long before you notice the beautiful, liquid song of the blue rock thrush. This delightful bird sits high on a rocky crag for a vantage point and sings its heart out. The aptly named crag

As its name suggests, the giant orchid is the largest member of the family found on the Balearics. It flowers in early spring

PEACE AND QUIET

martin also frequents similar habitat and nests on precipitous ledges.

Good mountain scenery and wildlife can be seen along the road from Puerto de Pollença to Soller, passing Puig Tomir. Visitors can also double back and drive south to Inca. There are numerous mountain walks in the area – ask at the tourist office for details.

Agricultural Land

Much of the lowlands of the Balearics are used for agriculture. The land use varies from small scale farming to vineyards and elegant olive groves, but since much of the land is poor, stony soil it is often a wonder that anything grows at all.

The olive is only one of many introduced plants on the islands. The prickly pear, a large cactus introduced from the Americas, is widely encouraged as a hedging plant, and equally at home is the agave or century plant, with its huge spiny rosette of leaves and towering flower spike.

A few native plants also seem to thrive in the parched and disturbed agricultural environment. Most noticeable is the ubiquitous asphodel, *asphodelus microcarpus*, a true indicator of disturbed and often overgrazed habitat. In the spring the flower spikes of the tassel hyacinth blow in the wind, and around the field edges plants such as the starry clover, with its star-shaped seed heads, somehow manage to survive.

In sandy areas, and particularly where irrigation takes place, mole crickets can be quite numerous. Although chiefly subterranean creatures, which use their enlarged forelegs to burrow through the soil, they can sometimes be seen crawling across paths and tracks. Mole crickets burrow with extreme ease but have to be quick if they are to evade the beady eye of the woodchat shrike. This summer visitor to the Balearics catches insects which it impales on thorns or barbed wire while feeding, and is a common sight on fences and wires.

Short-toed larks and tawny pipits commonly feed in stony fields searching for insects and seeds and the fortunate observer may even see a stone curlew. These shy birds are mainly nocturnal but are often seen at dawn and dusk when they utter their strange, wailing calls. The most striking bird of the fields in the Balearics must be the hoopoe. Named after its repetitive song, its striking black and white markings are most clearly visible as it flies, looking like a giant moth.

Spring Flowers

The Balearics can boast a list of nearly 1,300 species of flowering plants – an immense number; and of these species, more than half flower in the spring, so that during even a short visit to the islands there will be plenty to see.

By growing in the autumn and winter and flowering in the

spring, Mediterranean plants produce seeds along before the heat of the summer. From June onwards, annual plants die off and the parts of perennial plants above ground wither and die back. In this way the plants do not have to contend with the

The familiar dwarf fan palm's presence is a good indicator of habitat where orchids and endemic flowers may be found

problems of dessication. Spring comes early in the Balearics, and one of the first flowers to herald its arrival is the giant orchid. The immense flower spike can sometimes be seen as early as February, usually in woodland glades and along shady roadside verges. Although spectacular in itself, it is just the forerunner of the orchids that appear in March, April and May. Coastal

woodland and scrub can be excellent for tongue orchids, the beautiful violet limodore and the naked man orchid, with its flowers shaped like little people.

Almost any sort of habitat that is not too disturbed will harbour a variety of species in the bee orchid family. All of them have flowers with flattened lower lips which have evolved to mimic bees and wasps. The aim of this deception is to attract the insects to what they think is a member of the opposite sex; instead of which, all they find is an unresponsive flower, but they unwittingly transport pollen from one plant to another. The most frequently encountered species include the Venus orchid, whose flowers have shiny, metallic patches; the aptly named sombre bee orchid, and the sawfly orchid.

Other spring flowers are less specialised in structure but are generally much more showy and colourful. The most conspicuous group is that of the rock-roses, with flowers that look like crushed crêpe paper. For displays of wild flowers, try the meadows between Alcudia to Artá. Look for orchids around Porto Colóm, beneath the pines near Albufera and beside the road to Cabo Formentor.

Mallorca's Endemic Flowers

Of the 1,300 species of plant found on the island of Mallorca, 40 are found nowhere else in the world

(these are called 'endemics') and there are also many other flowers that are significantly different from their counterparts on mainland Europe.

Although some of the endemic flowers are found in a variety of habitats across the island, the majority occur in a very precise type of habitat called the 'Balearic' zone. It is characterised by its stony, *garigue* appearance but the key feature, and one that is readily identifiable, is the presence of the Balearics' only native palm, the dwarf fan or *palmeto*. Wherever you see this plant you are likely to find some of the endemic flowers.

The Formentor peninsula in the extreme north of Mallorca is a particularly rewarding place to search. The scenery is staggeringly beautiful, with immense knife-edge cliffs dropping into deep blue seas. Because of its scenic beauty, there are many stopping-off points before you reach the lighthouse at Cabo Formentor, and all are good points from which to explore the surrounding land. The ground on either side of the tunnel on the road to Formentor has many endemic plants and other interesting flowers, such as Berteloni's bee orchid. It is also a good spot to look for the tiny Marmora's warbler.

The most frequently seen, but most commonly overlooked endemic flower must be the St John's wort, *hypericum balearicum*. Thousands of people drive past it each week on their way to Formentor and

Bee-eaters are undoubtedly the most colourful birds of the Balearics, arriving in April

few realise that the yellow flowers growing almost out of the tarmac beside the road belong to one of the world's rarest plants! A short walk from any of the parking spots on the road to Formentor, or from the lighthouse itself, should enable you to find the 'hedgehog'-shaped milk vetch *astragalus poterium*, patches of cyclamen, *cyclamen balearicum* and the native paeony, *paeonia cambessedesii*. You should also look out for a little plant which looks like a small, white daisy growing among the rocks: this is *senecio rodriguezei*. It lacks an English name but has been nick-named 'Roddy's flower' by visiting botanists!

Bird Migration in the Balearics

Many European birds journey to and from Africa each year to escape the ravages of the northern winter. Each time they make the trip they all face a common obstacle: the Mediterranean.

Although some birds use the land-bridges at either end of the Mediterranean, many get blown off course and some species intentionally fly directly over the sea. The Balearic Islands, lying as they do in the middle of the Mediterranean, are an important stopping-off point for tired migrants.

Spring migration in the Balearics, from March to May, is more impressive than the autumn migration. Migrants pass through the islands

PEACE AND QUIET

throughout the spring and colourful parties of bee-eaters occur on a daily basis. However, under certain weather conditions exceptional numbers of birds can appear overnight.

Birds are encouraged to attempt the crossing of the Mediterranean when there is a tail wind from the south or southwest, and many do so only at night. If the wind suddenly changes direction overnight, or a cold front passes through, then a 'fall' of birds will occur with thousands of birds involved. These migrant birds will feed up for a day or so and then resume their migration when the weather improves.

Tired migrants do not land just anywhere, but rather each species tries to find the habitat that most suits it. So, passerine birds are found in arable fields and scrub, and waders, terns and swallows over the marshes. This rule is not absolute by any means, but certainly holds true in most cases.

After a large 'fall' it is always worth checking the common species for something more unusual. For example, red-throated pipits are regularly seen among meadow pipits, and similarly black-eared wheatears can be found among common wheatears. The fields around Casas Veyas in Mallorca are noted for migrants, as is the area around the lighthouse on Formentor. Casas Veyas can be found beside the road between Puerto de Pollença and Cabo

Formentor. In spring, there may be several birdwatching groups in the area. An informal gathering of birdwatchers usually takes place once a week in one of the Puerto de Pollença hotels to discuss 'what's around'.

The Salinas

For centuries, salt has been an essential part of Mediterranean life; at one time it was even used as a form of currency, such was its worth. The traditional method of extracting salt from seawater still persists and huge saltpans or *salinas*, such as those at Salinas de Levante on Mallorca, are a familiar sight. Shallow lagoons are flooded with seawater and the sun evaporates the water, leaving pure salt.

Saltpans and the high salinity water they contain provide ideal conditions for brine shrimps, which in turn become food for wading birds. The black-winged stilt is the most characteristic bird of the saltpans, with its smart black and white plumage and ridiculously long, red legs. They frequently nest on the embankments around the saltpans, and it is rather comical to watch them try to settle on their nests. Their legs, so well suited to wading in deep water, are a real encumbrance when they try to settle on their eggs.

For Salinas de Levante, drive to Petra in the south, follow signs to Vila Franca; at Campos, follow signs to Colonia Sant Jordí.

ACCOMMODATION

There are close on 1,750 hotels in the Balearic Islands and you can expect the full range of services. All of them are classified according to a star system that goes from one-star to five-star – the luxury class. The rating is imposed by government inspectors and it relates to the services and facilities that each establishment offers, so you should know straight away what to expect.

At a one-star hotel there must be a bathroom for every seven rooms, a washbasin in 50 per cent of the rooms and a shower and washbasin in 25 per cent of the rooms. There should be a lift if there are more than four floors, a telephone on every floor and a laundry service.

At a two-star establishment there must be a common bathroom for every six rooms, a shower and washbasin in 45 per cent of the rooms, a washbasin in 40 per cent of them and a complete bathroom in the remaining 15 per cent. There should be a lift if there are more than three floors, a telephone in every room and a bar.

A three-star establishment must provide a bath in 50 per cent of its rooms, a shower in

The distinctive and delicate design which is characteristic of a Mallorcan courtyard

ACCOMMODATION/FOOD AND DRINK

the other half and a washbasin and toilet in every room. It should also have a lift as well as a bar, a lobby and a telephone in every room.
A four-star establishment ensures a complete bathroom for 75 per cent of the rooms, a shower, washbasin and toilet in 25 per cent of them and air conditioning in common rooms and bedrooms. It should also have a garage if it is in a city, at least two lobbies and a bar. To obtain a five-star hotel rating a hotel must have complete bathrooms in every bedroom, several lobbies, suites and a number of facilities such as hairdressers. Hotel prices are regulated by the Tourist Authorities according to the star rating and will be clearly visible at the reception desk and also in your room. You should note that some prices include VAT, which is known as IVA in Spain (6 per cent, rising to 15 per cent in five-star hotels), in the total charge while others do not and this should be specified on the rate card in the lobby and on the individual price sheet in your room.

FOOD AND DRINK

It is possible, of course, to eat at the Balearic resorts exactly the same food that you are used to back home; an alternative is to try the local cooking. Balearic cuisine is essentially Mediterranean. It makes full use of local herbs and of tomatoes, aubergines, courgettes, and peppers. These are all fried up together

and form the basis for a variety of fish stews.
Caldereta (which means stew) *de langosta* has the local red lobster as its main ingredient. *Caldereta de peix* (meaning fish) is the same sort of hearty stew, using whatever came in with the catch, fish and seafood mixed together.
You are certain to come across two local specialities: *ensaimadas*, which are the local fluffy and light pastries and *sobrasada*, which is a red spicy sausage paté. *Sopas Mallorquinas* are very thick soups with chunky bits of bread floating about in them and *empanadillas* are mini-pies and can be either sweet or savoury.
Paella is not a Balearic dish, for it comes from the Valencia region, and nor is the cold tomato soup called *gazpacho* that originated from the southern Spanish region of Andalucia. Both, however, are on just about every restaurant menu in the Balearics, as they are everywhere else in Spain. Mistrust instantly a quickly made, fast food *paella*. For this rice dish to be cooked properly, you will have to wait a good half hour.
One of the oddest dishes you are likely to encounter is *Calamares en su tinta* which is squid cut usually in rings and stewed in its own ink and is, of course, jet black. It is invariably served with white rice and most people find it delicious. *Calamares a la Romana* are rings of squid fried in batter (anything that is *a la Romana* is batter fried).

Seafood is, naturally, the basis of many Balearic dishes. This catch is on display in Mahón market

Shrimp, *gambas*, can come *a la parilla* (grilled), *al ajilla* (fried in garlic) or *a la Romana*, which is the sort of scampi dish that many people are more familiar with.

Olive Oil
Your stomach may object to olive oil, which is doubly unfortunate, for olive oil is universally used in Spanish cooking and it also happens to be healthy. If you have to avoid olive oil ask for dishes that are *a la parilla*, meaning grilled, or that are baked in the oven and described as *al horna* or *asado*. *Frito* means fried, inevitably in olive oil.

Spicy Food
Garlic is called *ajo* and if you don't like it, say *No ajo* to the waiter and you will be understood. Spanish food, as a rule, is not spicy and should not be confused with Mexican food, which is. Spicy is *picante* and a dish will generally be described as such if it is hot. To be quite sure ask the waiter: *Es* (is it) *picante?*

Wines and Liqueurs
The Balearics do produce wine, but there is not much of it and it is not very good. Virtually all the wine that is drunk is imported from mainland Spain. The classy, and the best known, Spanish red wine comes from the Rioja region; everyday red plonk has *Valdepeñas* printed on the label. A wine that says *Reserva* on the label has been aged at least three years in a barrel and is priced up accordingly. Catalonian wines, grown in the district called Penedés, are up-

FOOD AND DRINK

market and good. Some of these wines – there are reds, whites and rosés – have a deservedly high reputation. The Catalan sparkling wine is called *Cava* and it comes as *seco*, dry, *dulce*, sweet or *semi-seco*, which is the halfway house. It is made following the champagne producing method and it has more to do with French bubbly than the Italian sparkling wines. It you see white wines from the Rueda region (north central Spain) on a wine list, go for them. Likewise, go for the rosés produced in Cigales and the reds produced in the region called La Ribera del Duero, which are Rioja areas. These wines are the sort that are less known outside Spain, because the domestic market drinks up all that is available. Sherry is, surprisingly perhaps, hardly drunk in Spain outside the Jerez district of southern Spain, where it is produced. Sweet and cream sherries are virtually unknown in Spain and if sherry is drunk at all it is *fino*, pale and dry, and it is served well chilled. In the liqueur department you will come across Spanish brandy, called *Cognac*, which can be quite rough, unless you choose the more expensive brands, and an aniseed-type drink called *Anís* which also packs a punch. A drink called *Pacharán*, not too unlike sloe gin, is also very popular and is usually served with ice. The Balearic Islands do produce a variety of herb-based liqueurs called *Licor de Hierbas* which are very popular. The bottles are eye-catching because they have the herbs inside the bottle and the liquid is normally of a marvellous green tint. In Menorca a local gin, *Ginebra*, is manufactured, a legacy of the 18th-century period when the island was ruled by Britain.

Drinking

There are no restrictions in Spain about when it is legal to

Seaside snacks on Ibiza

FOOD AND DRINK

drink in public establishments. Bars open in the morning, sometimes very early, and can close at dawn or even stay open all night: it depends on the owner and his employees.

Be warned that spirits are served in Spain in amounts that would be classified in some other countries as much more generous measures. Learn the local Spanish habit of nibbling *tapas* while you drink in a bar. It is an insurance against losing control.

Spaniards love their drink but are rarely overtly drunk and the *tapa* practice obviously has something to do with this restraint.

Water

Tap water is generally good, but it is best to go for bottled mineral water, to be on the safe side. Bubbly mineral water is called *agua con gas*, and still mineral water is called *agua sin gas*. Bottled mineral water is available in all bars, restaurants and supermarkets.

SHOPPING

One of the cheapest genuine souvenirs to bring home from the Balearics, and certainly the most unusual and the most easily carried, is a hand-made clay whistle. Once upon a time they were used by shepherds, then by children as toys and nowadays they are made and sold as popular decorative objects. They are called *siruells* and they are normally fashioned into the shape of the human head, although you will also come across bull and horse shaped *siruells*. You will find them in most handicraft shops and particularly in the Old Quarter, the *Barrio Antiguo* of Palma de Mallorca.

Clay modelling has a long tradition on the islands and similar popular inexpensive art objects include reproductions of typical peasant houses in the Balearics. For a little extra cost you can have a short message painted on the models.

At the other end of the scale, Mallorca is the home of cultured pearls, which are considerably less expensive than the real oyster product but are by no means cheap. Buy the cultured pearls that are accompanied by the relevant guarantee; it is best to buy them in Manacor, or try jewellery shops in Palma de Mallorca's Calle de Plateria, near Plaza Santa Eulalia.

Embroidery and fabrics have long been Mallorcan

Good ceramics are often to be found in local workshops – or in displays such as this, in Manacor

handicrafts. They are not cheap, either, but they are the genuine article. You will find good fabric shops on the central Calle Conquistador in Palma de Mallorca. This same street has boutiques selling high quality leather work and

Basket weaving and products made from *esparto* grass and rope make up a different sector of Balearic handicrafts, and a very large one it is too. There is an immense variety of sandals, straw hats, shoulder bags and, of course, baskets themselves in all shapes and sizes. You will find tourist shops crammed with such objects and the quality is inevitably uneven.

Fun footwear for use on your holiday and to show off back home are the rope-soled sandals that are known as espadrilles and called *alpargatas* in Spanish. The genuine, old-style ones are open, with strips of linen covering the toe and the heel and with long linen laces to strap up your leg, Roman style.

The town of Eivissa is every bit as much of a shopping paradise as is Palma de Mallorca. It is also rather more zany and avante-garde. You will find an abundance of leatherwork, of costume jewellery and of hand painted T-shirts to suit every taste.

In Ibiza there are scores of boutiques and the rage there is the so-called Ad Lib fashion.

Ad Lib is a generic term for a line of casual, and not always expensive, clothes that are roomy and comfortable and owe their inspiration to traditional Ibizan costumes.

In the food and drink department you won't go

contemporary jewellery. Traditional Mallorcan jewellery, consisting of gold and silver earrings and cords of gold braid once used to decorate clothing, has been adapted to modern designs, and you can find unusual and appealing objects which will often be considerably cheaper than those which you would find back home.

far in the Balearics without encountering the large local pastry buns that are called *ensaimadas* and the spicy sausage called *sobrasada* that looks rather like a paté and is spread on bread.

You might have difficulties getting these foodstuffs back home through the customs but you will have no trouble in returning with a bottle of the Balearics herb liqueur which is called *Licor de Hierbas*. This liqueur is aniseed based and packs a powerful punch.

WEATHER AND WHEN TO GO

Sun Most people are lured to Spain by the promise of non-stop sun, and this means that most people need to be warned about sun stroke. Keep your head covered, use tanning lotions and potions with a high protection factor, let your skin accustom itself gradually to the sun and wear sun-glasses. Take extra

Cooling off in the Son Bou resort's Club San Jaime, on Menorca

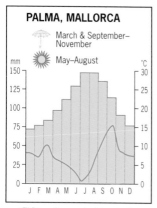

PALMA, MALLORCA

March & September–November

May–August

and eight days of rain. Averages for that month in Ibiza are 15°C (59°F) maximum, 8°C (46°F) minimum and seven days of rain. The statistics for Mahón, Menorca, are 13°C (55°F) maximum, 7°C (45°F) minimum and 10 rainy days. In July expect 29°C (84°F) maximum and 19°C (66°F) minimum in Palma, 29°C (84°F) maximum, 20°C (68°F) minimum in Ibiza and 28°C (82°F) maximum, 20°C (68°F) minimum in Mahón. Average July rainfall in the Balearics is 4mm.

special care of children and ensure, at all times, that they are wearing something on their heads.

Sea The Mediterranean is not, as a rule, rough and, on the whole, there are no dangerous undertows and currents. Nevertheless, take sensible precautions: don't swim immediately after heavy meals and don't swim out too far. Windsurfers, and yachtsmen generally, should also note that the breezes can be deceptively light.

The rule of thumb is that Menorca is somewhat wetter and cooler in winter and that Ibiza is slightly drier and warmer. In summer there is very little to choose, weatherwise, between the three islands. Mallorca and Menorca total an average of 2,600 hours of sunlight a year and Ibiza has 2,900.

In January expect maximum temperatures of 14°C (57°F) in Palma, minimum temperatures of 6°C (43°F)

HOW TO BE A LOCAL

There are parts of the Balearic Islands where locals are so thin on the ground that the best way to fit in is to be a tourist like everybody else. That said, you will find it pleasurably surprising how much a little courtesy and general friendliness is appreciated by the locals.

Islanders will quickly respond to a gesture on your part – *bondia* (good morning), *bon tarde* (good afternoon) and *s'es plau* (please) – will enlist a good response as you are attempting the local language (ancient Catalan) which the islanders are very proud of.

Spaniards are as a rule courteous and friendly, happy to receive visitors and pleased when their services are appreciated. Drunkards, for example, are loathed in Spain so too, are litterlouts.

Though Spain used to keep late hours for dining, these days most places do not serve cooked food after 14.25hrs at lunchtime and 21.30hrs in the evening.

An afternoon siesta from 15.00–17.00hrs is a sensible custom to avoid the extreme heat. In the towns, away from the beach, try to be correctly dressed, the locals are always smartly dressed whatever the temperature.

CHILDREN

Children should be the least of your worries if you are travelling in Spain. Spaniards really do love children and are constantly making a fuss of them. You can take them to bars, restaurants – anywhere; and if your baby starts wailing away, the waiter will as likely as not pat the child on the head and congratulate you on its good lungs.

Most hotels geared to the tourist trade have some sort of children's entertainment programme and also run a babysitting service. Most resorts have nearby a funfair, an aquapark or some similar facility for the special children's day out.

Obviously you have to be careful with the sun, with the exhaustion brought on by hours spent on the beach and with the dislocation children undergo through a change of diet and environment. Invariably children adapt perfectly well if their parents just act sensibly.

TIGHT BUDGET

●   One of the easiest ways of controlling your budget is to replace meals with *tapas*, the cooked snacks that you will find in every bar; or try the *bocadillos* – a selection of filled rolls. If you do want a full meal stick to the *menu del dia* (menu of the day), which is a set price, three course meal that every restaurant must by law provide.

●   An obviously cheaper alternative is to go to the local town supermarket (avoid the resort supermarkets which are far more expensive) and buy provisions. Stock up on fruit, which is plentiful and cheap, and on *sobrasada*, which is a local spicy red sausage that looks like paté. Spread *sobrasada* thickly on bread and you will find it a meal in itself.

●   Another home grown sandwich variation is *pan con tomate* (bread and tomato). The local way of doing it is to rub the French loaf with a clove of garlic, pulp and squeeze the tomato into the bread and then sprinkle salt over it. If you add a slice of home cured ham (*jamón serrano*) to the tomato sandwich then you have a complete meal.

●   As a general rule, the *vino de la casa* (house wine) is a good bet for a reasonable wine at a reasonable price. All wine is now imported, as the island vineyards were greatly affected by phylloxera at the end of the last century.

●   For phone calls use 'cabins' – far cheaper than hotel phones.

*'Fill her up, please'... local
transport reflects the slow pace
which still exists in parts of
Mallorca*

DIRECTORY

Arriving

Airports Flights into Mallorca
land at Son San Joan airport, 7
miles (11km) from the centre of
Palma de Mallorca. Son San
Joan is a large airport and
during the summer it is one of
the busiest in Europe (tel:
264624).
Flights into Ibiza land at Es
Codolar airport 5½ miles
(9km) from Eivissa (Ibiza
town). Most of the traffic
consists of charter flights (tel:
302200).
Flights into Menorca land at
San Clemente airport, 3 miles
(5km) from Mahón. (tel:
360150). Formentera has no
airport. Most of its visitors
arrive at Ibiza and then take
the ferry or hydrofoil.
All the airports except Minorca
are served by buses to the
capitals of the respective
islands and there are also
regular bus services to
specific resorts and locations
on the island. Taxis have a
fixed fare to the city centre and
to other towns on the islands. If
you choose to take a taxi make
sure you check the fixed fare
with the driver before you hire
his services.

Camping

Under Spanish law camping is
not permitted on beaches or
on river shores, in the
mountains, within half a mile
(1km) of a town, 164 yards
(150m) of a water supply, 110
yards (100m) of a national
monument or 55 yards (50m)

of a public highway.
Otherwise you may camp
where you like except that you
will need the permission of the
owner if you are camping on
private property and that, of
course, means practically
everywhere. For information
and booking contact the
Spanish Camping Federation
(Federación Española de
Empresarios de Campings y
Ciudades de Vacaciones),
General Oráa 52–2°D, 28006
Madrid (tel: (91) 562–9994).

Car Breakdowns
The procedure if you are
unlucky enough to have a
breakdown is to contact the
nearest *taller*, Spanish for
garage, which has full
breakdown facilities. There
are *talleres* in every small
town, usually at the entrance,
and you are likely to find that
Spanish mechanics are skilful
and efficient.

Car Hire
All the major car hire brand
names will be urging their
vehicles on you from the
moment you arrive. There are
also a great number of local
hire firms, which should in no
way be disparaged. Demand
advice, if you need it, from
your travel agent.
The big advantage of car hire
in the Balearics is that it
enables you to reach the out of
the way coves and semi-
private beaches that are the
real ornament of the
archipelago. The necessity of
real caution when driving on
unknown Spanish roads
cannot be stressed enough.

Chemist see **Pharmacist**.

Crime
The Balearic Islands are neither
more, nor especially less,
dangerous than anywhere else.
Whatever you do, do not leave
anything visible and unattended
in your car. There is a very high
probability that it will be stolen
and this includes the car radio.
Muggings are on the increase,
so don't walk around with a lot
of money or credit cards, and
keep your documents in your
hotel. If you are unfortunate
enough to be mugged, do not
try any heroics: muggers are
often heroin addicts and
dangerous.
You should leave cash and
valuables in the hotel safe.
Whatever you may have read
about Spain being soft on
drugs, forget it. Smuggling and
dealing can land you in prison
for six years, and small amounts
of drugs for personal use can
also cause a lot of trouble. Spain
as a whole does have a serious
drug problem and in fact 80 per
cent of all crime is reckoned to
be drug-related.
Spaniards and normal tourists
are beginning to get fed up with
holiday rowdiness. Drunken, or
just over-boisterous, youths
creating what others might
construe as a disturbance can
earn themselves, at least, a
crack from a truncheon and a
night in jail. Spaniards can be
the world's most hospitable
people, but they have also
started to be selective about
whom they want visiting them.
If you should fall foul of the law,
ask to speak to your consul:
Quiero hablar con (I want to

speak with) *el Consul.* Whatever you do keep calm, be polite and don't let yourself be provoked. Words like *por favor* (please) *gracias* (thank you) and *perdón* (sorry) are

Taking to the road can be an excellent way of leaving the bustle of the resorts behind

always useful.

Customer Complaints

Hotels, camping sites, restaurants, bars and discos have by law to provide official complaints forms, which are called *Hojas de Reclamacin.* Feel free to use them if you think there is cause to.

DIRECTORY

Other complaints such as an avaricious taxi driver who is charging far too much, should be lodged at the town council, the *Ayuntamiento*. Make sure you have all the necessary information, such as the number of the taxi cab.

Customs Regulations

You must have a valid passport, but visas are not necessary for most foreign nationals nor for EC citizens for a stay of up to 90 days.

The amount of alcohol and tobacco you can arrive with varies according to the country from which you are travelling. You may import or export unrestricted amounts of currency, provided amounts in excess of 1,000,000 pesetas, or its equivalent in foreign currency, are declared on arrival in Spain. You must also arrive with a minimum of 5,000 pesatas per day, or a total of 50,000 pesatas, unless you are on a package holiday.

Domestic Travel

Buses If you want to explore and to mingle with the natives, hop on a bus. The normal method of getting from A to B on the Balearics if you are not a car or yacht owner is to head for the *autobús*, and every helpful native will tell you where the local bus station, *estación de autobúses*, is to be found. Remember to check the time of the last bus home.

Rail If you want to travel by rail through Mallorca take the slow, narrow gauge train from Palma to Sóller. It is a nice trip,

A tram rumbles along the edge of the sands in Puerto de Sóller

crossing the island via almond and olive groves from north to south. The Balearics only other railway line is from Palma to Inca.

Taxis Taxis are usually white and have a horizontal stripe and 'taxi' clearly written on the side. A blue sign with a 'T' on it indicates a taxi rank. A taxi that is for hire will say *Libre*, either on a notice by the windshield or on the roof of the cab. At night a green pilot light also indicates that it is for hire. There are scalphunters everywhere. Check that the taxi driver has lowered his meter just as soon as you enter the cab. A properly registered cab should have a meter that is clearly visible. Beware of *aficionado* taxi drivers.

There will be extras to pay, in a properly registered cab, if you are being driven into town from the airport, if you have lots of luggage aboard and if it is a weekend or public holiday or late at night. These extras are printed out on a card which every cabbie has with him, and you have every right to peruse the additional fares.

Out of town trips by taxi have a set fee, so ask what it is before you set off and agree on the price. It is normal to tip taxi drivers between 25 and 75 pesetas, depending on the length of the trip.

Driving Take a lot of care when you drive in Spain. If you haven't travelled to, say, Morocco or Portugal, you will soon come to the conclusion that Spaniards are the worst drivers you have ever seen. You will need to be extra careful when motoring in

Spain; remember you will be driving on the right.

If an oncoming driver on the highway flashes his headlights at you, it is likely to mean that a few miles or kilometres up the road there is a *Guardia Civil* police trap on the look-out for speeding, unlawful overtaking or plain shoddy driving. This friendly warning system is widely practised among Spaniards.

Flashing headlights at a cross roads in a built up area do not, in Spain, mean: 'I am giving way to you'. They mean the opposite: 'out of the way'.

There are not, as yet, spot drinking and driving checks. Any accident will, however, invariably involve a breathalyser/urine/blood count, and evidence of alcohol considerably increases judicial severity. The moral is to do as you would at home. Remember that a shot of spirits in Spain may be the equivalent of a large triple in your country.

Ferries The main inter-island and island-to-mainland Spain ferry company is Trasmediterránea. The company has offices at Palma de Mallorca (Paseo Muelle Viejo 5, tel: 726740), at Ibiza (Avenida Bartolomé Vicente Ramós 1, tel: 315011) and at Mahón (Nuevo Muelle Comercial, tel: 366050).

Roads The roads of mountainous northwest Mallorca combine steep gradients with hairpin bends. Menorca has only one main road, from Mahón to Ciudadela, and virtually no coastal roads. Ibiza's roads are also narrow and twisting. The only stretch of motorway is a ring road around Palma while a main carriageway extends from Palma to Andraitx.

Electricity
220v-225v is the norm. Many hotels also provide a 110v-125v special socket for shavers. As two round pins are used, an adaptor is necessary for British and American appliances.

Embassies and Consulates
UK Consulates
Mallorca: Plaza Mayor 3, Palma de Mallorca (tel: 712445).
Menorca: Torret 28, San Luis (tel: 366439).
Ibiza: Avenida Isidoro Macabich 45, Eivissa (tel: 301818).
US Consulates
Mallorca: Avenida Rey Jaime III

26, Palma de Mallorca (tel: 722660).
Menorca: See Mallorca.
The Canadian Embassy is at Calle Nunêz de Balboa 35, Madrid (tel: 91 431 4300).

Emergency Telephone Numbers
Dial 003 for the operator and ask for *Policía* (police), *Bomberos* (fire service) or *Cruz Roja* (Red Cross).

Entertainment Information
Every main town will have its local *Oficina de Turismo* (Tourist Office) which is invariably

Scaling the heights to trim the palm trees in the Mallorcan village of Petra (see page 50)

A Manacor pearl factory: cultured pearls are a Mallorcan speciality

centrally located and is there to provide full information on what's on and where to go.

Health

British visitors to Spain benefit from free medical treatment on production of Form E111 (available from British post offices). It is also advisable (essential for non-EC citizens) to have private medical insurance.

Holidays (Public and Religious)

There are many local variations as each town and village has its own feast days. National public holidays include 25 December, 1 January, 6 January, 19 March, Good Friday, Easter Monday, 1 May, 24 June, Corpus Christi, 29 June, 25 July, 15 August, 12 October, 1 November and 8 December. Though these are public holidays restaurants and bars remain open. Banks and shops do close, however.

Lost Property

Enquire at the *Ayuntamiento* (the Town Hall).

Money Matters

Spain's currency is the peseta. There are 1, 5, 10, 25, 50, 100, 200 and 500 peseta coins and there are 1,000, 2,000, 5,000 and 10,000 peseta notes. All major credit cards are operative in Spain and are used extensively. Use a bank to change money, as hotels mark up on the official exchange rate.

DIRECTORY

Opening Times

Shops generally open Monday to Saturday at about 09.00, and quite often close for a lunch break between 13.00 and 17.00. They usually remain open until 20.00.

The normal banking hours are 08.30 to 14.00 Monday to Saturday (closed Saturdays June to September). It is worth checking with your local bank, as some branches open in the afternoon and others remain closed on Saturdays.

The Balearics, geared as they are for the foreign visitor, do offer the visitor a choice of European or of Spanish hours. Even so don't expect to get lunch before 13.00 nor dinner before 21.30 hrs.

You may well be surprised by the hours that Spaniards keep. If you stick to your year-round eating schedule you are likely to be permanently out of joint. In Spain, if it is winter, people sit down for luncheon sometime between 14.00 and 15.00 and in summer at about 15.00 or 16.00. Then, if it is a holiday period, there is a well-earned siesta. Spaniards gather at mid-morning, which can be at any time between 10.00 and 14.00, for late breakfasts and/or pre-lunch *aperitivos*, meaning drinks and *tapas*. Dinner can start any time after 21.30 and peak hours are around 23.00.

Ibiza's windmills take advantage of the hot African winds which sometimes blow over the island

Personal Safety

Take normal precautions. Don't leave anything visible in a parked car; preferably don't leave anything in it at all. Only carry on you the amount of cash you are likely to need and use the hotel safe to store valuables. There are pickpockets and muggers about. Women are well advised not to hitchhike alone.

Pharmacist

A chemist is called a *Farmacia* and there will always be one in the vicinity running a 24-hour service. Printed lists at the entrance to a *Farmacia* will tell you which chemist happens to be on duty. In Spain a great deal can be bought over the counter that would require a prescription elsewhere.

Places of Worship

Spain is predominantly a Roman Catholic country and Catholic churches are everywhere. Enquire at your hotel or the tourist information office for services conducted by other denominations.

Police

Spain has three types of uniformed, armed policemen. The *Guardia Civil* wear green uniforms and they will be checking your luggage at the customs on arrival. They are also the traffic police and patrol the roads on their huge motorbikes. Sometimes they will wear their traditional tricorned patent leather hats, but more often nowadays they wear peaked grey caps. You will also meet the *Policía Nacional*, in brown uniforms and berets, on arrival because

this corps is responsible for stamping your passport. The *Policía Nacional* duties include urban policing in cities and towns while the *Guardia Civil* is in charge of the law in small villages and rural areas. Finally, town councils run their own *Policía Municipal*, in blue uniforms, who are responsible for traffic control. Some resorts, especially those which have experienced hooliganism, have special security services that keep an eye on potential bar wreckers. For police help in a town ask for *La Comisaría*, the police stations run by the *Policía Nacional*. Out of town ask for *El Cuartel de la Guardia Civil*, the Civil Guard barracks.

Post Office

There are not that many post offices around. The job of selling stamps (*sellos*) is also done by shops or booths called *estancos*. These are also stationery shops and they double up as tobacconists, selling cigarettes at the official rate – far cheaper than in bars, restaurants and hotels.
If you want to send telegrams, parcels, giros, telefaxes, etc, and you are not near a well run hotel, it is best to ask where the local post office, *oficina de correos*, is located.

Poste Restante

To receive *Poste Restante* mail, ask the sender to write *Poste Restante* or *Lista de Correos* on the envelope, and make sure you have a document of identification such as a passport to show when you go to pick up your mail. Post boxes in Spain are painted yellow.

The magic of the Balearic Islands: sunset at Santa Ponsa

Senior Citizens/Student Travel

On mainland Spain some Senior Citizens may be able to apply for railway reductions on presentation of their own equivalent card. Young people under 26 years may apply for Eurorail passes or a *Tarjeta Joven*, (youth card) for 50 per cent discounts on fares. In the Balearics there are no specific breaks for either group.

Telephones

All you need to make an international call is a good supply of 100 or 500 peseta coins and a non-vandalised booth. Do not press the button to the left of the dial, or you may lose your money. All international calls involve dialling first 07 and then, after the tone changes, dialling the country code, which should be clearly marked alongside the headset, followed by the area code (without the initial 0) and your number.

Hotel calls usually incur a surcharge, so public booths and, better still, the local telephone offices – ask for *las oficinas de telefónica* – are to be recommended. An advantage of the latter is that you pay after your call and do not have to save up loose change. Calls at weekends and at night are cheaper. Dial 9398 for numbers in Europe, and 9391 for other international numbers. Dial 003 for local directory enquiries.

Time
Spain is one hour ahead of GMT and two hours ahead from late March to September.

Tipping
In bars and restaurants, tip between 5 and 10 per cent of what you are charged. Remember that in a bar you pay at the end, not after every round of drinks. Taxi drivers expect between 25 and 75 pesetas, and hotel staff will happily accept 50 to 100 pesetas for services such as finding you a taxi or carrying your bags around the place.

Toilets
Public toilets, you will find, are few and far between but this is no problem, for you can use the washroom of any bar or cafeteria.

Most bar owners will not be bothered if you walk in from the street for that specific purpose.

Tourist Offices
The Balearic Tourism Council (*Conselleria de Turisme de Balears*), the main tourist body governing the islands, is at Avenida Rey Jaime III 10, Palma de Mallorca (tel: 712216). On Menorca the main office is at Plaza Explanada 40, Mahón (tel: 363790); Ibiza it is at Paseo Vara de Rey 13, Eivissa (tel: 301900); and Formentera at Port de la Savina (tel: 322057). There are also local official tourist offices called *oficinas de turismo*. Enquire at the local town Hall, the *Ayuntamiento*.

Travel Agencies
There is a host of travel agencies everywhere on the Balearics, offering trips, entertainment excursions and all other facilities to make your holiday complete. You can shop around for what suits you best.

LANGUAGE

yes sí
no no
please por favor
thank you gracias
good morning buenos días
good night buenas noches
I want quiero
I am looking for busco
where is dónde está
how much cuánto es
airport aeropuerto
beach playa
hotel hotel
restaurant restaurante
beer cerveza
wine vino

INDEX

ACKNOWLEDGEMENTS

ACKNOWLEDGEMENTS
The Automobile Association would like to thank the following photographers and libraries for their assistance in the compilation of this book

J ALLAN CASH PHOTOLIBRARY 49 Porto Colóm, 58/9 Ciudadela, 66/7 Eivissa, 68 Old Town, 84 San Miguel, 112 Son Bou, 120 Petra.

INTERNATIONAL PHOTOBANK Cover Cala Fornells, 6/7 Windsurfing, 8 Shopping, 11 Es Cona, 13 Sóller, 20/1 Palma harbour, 23 Bellver Castle, 26/7 Palacio Almudaina, 31 Magaluf beach, 36 Valldemossa, 44 Paguera, 51 San Parc, 52 Nr Villacarlos, 56 Villacarlos, 61 Santa Galdana, 63 Santa Eulalia del Rio, 65 Eivissa, 70 The cathedral, 74/5 Café, 80 San Mateo, 83 Scenery, 87 Street cafés, 89 La Sabina, 90/1 Formentera, 105 Courtyard, 107 Mahón market, 108/9 Beach café, 110/1 Manacor, 115 Local transport, 122 Windmill.

NATURE PHOTOGRAPHERS LTD 92 Garigue habitat (A J Cleave), 94/5 Cory's shearwater (M Bolton), 96 Swallowtail (M Bolton), 97 Scop's Owl (M E Gore), 98 Hellebore, 99 Giant orchid, 101 Dwarf fan palm (A J Cleave), 103 Bee-eater (P R Sterry).

R SNELLING 72 La Marina, 67 Pottery.

SPECTRUM COLOUR LIBRARY 15 Drach caves, 16 Carthusian monastery, 28 Nightclub, 33 Deià, 34 Puerto de Sóller, 38 Cabo Formentor, 41 Pollença market, 42 Artá, 46 Santa Ponsa, 118 Tram, 121 Pearl factory, 124 Sunset.

ZEFA PICTURE LIBRARY (UK) LTD 4 Cala Mondrago, 17 Santa Ponsa, 55 Mahón, 79 Portinatx, 117 Taking to the road.

Thanks also to **Mona King** for her assistance with the revised edition

For this revision: Copy editor Jenny Fry; Verifier: Colin Follett